ISBN 978-1-5278-5693-6
PIBN 10890448

FB &c Ltd, Dalton House, 60 Windsor Avenue, London, SW19 2RR.
Company number 08720141. Registered in England and Wales.

For support please visit www.forgottenbooks.com

* * * *
* * * * *

A HISTORY OF HUNGARIAN MUSIC

* * * * *
* * * *
* * *
* *
*

Issued as a
"Musical Standard" Extra.

For List of Musical Works please refer to the end of the volume.

BY

JULIUS KALDY

(DIRECTOR OF THE ROYAL HUNGARIAN OPERA)

LONDON:
WILLIAM REEVES,
The "Musical Standard" Office,
83 Charing Cross Road, W.C.

This little work, issued as a MUSICAL STANDARD extra, is Reprinted from "The Millennium of Hungary and Its People,"* by permission of the Editor, Dr. Joseph de Jekelfalussy, Director of the Royal Hungarian Statistical Office and Ministerial Councillor.

* *Published under the authority of the Royal Hungarian Minister of Commerce. Budapest.*

Printed by
W. Reeves, 83 Charing Cross Road, London, W.C.

A HISTORY * * OF * * * HUNGARIAN MUSIC * * *

THE Hungarians must have had a special love for music in their original home, for in their sacrifices and other religious ceremonies, in their national festivals, before and after a battle, at banquets and funerals, Song, Music, and Dancing played an important rôle.

In religious sacrifices the High priest (Táltos) led the ceremony with Song. The people, repeating the last verse of the stanza, softly sang the refrain, and young girls, scattering fragrant herbs in the altar flame, danced a blithe dance. At national festivals and at banquets the minstrels sang, accompanying themselves on their lute, the heroic deeds of fallen champions, or poured forth other patriotic songs, while reciters declaimed in sonorous rhythms the old heroic legends.

Our ancestors used to inter their dead with song and music. Priests of lower rank (Gyulas) delivered an address at the funeral, praised the heroism and virtues of the dead, and at the end paced round the grave in a slow dance. This custom likewise remained partially until the present day. For at burials—with Catholic and Protestant alike—the Cantor takes leave of the dead in a mournful song. After the interment the mourners assemble with the sorrowing family at the funeral banquet. 160 years ago the "Dance of Death" used to be danced after this evening meal.

This was probably the oldest Hungarian dance, which our people here danced for hundreds of years as a remnant of heathen funeral rites. Among the compositions of the renowned Gipsy musician, Czinka Panna, there is a "Dance of Death" melody, of the first half of the 18th century.

That music and song were in great maturity already among the Huns is proved by the Travels of Priscus Rhetor whom the Emperor of Byzantium sent along with the Senator Maximus on an embassy to Attila.

Like the Gallic bards, the Vates, and the Skandinavian Skalds, the Hun minstrels not only stimulated the fighters to the combat but took part in the battle themselves. Many of them remained on the field of battle. In 451, on the eve of the bloody and desperate battle of Catalaunum, when Attila withdrew to his barricade of waggons, the dirges of the Huns echoed from there to the enemy's camp. Next day numberless lutes were found on the battle-field.

Later, at the time of the conquest of the land, in the 10th century, the music of the Hungarians must have been highly developed, for the "Anonymous" of King Béla (Anonymus Bélæ Regis notarius) ends his account of the fights of the leaders Lel, Bulcsu, and Botond, with the words: "As to their wars and heroic deeds, if you pay no credence to my letter, at least believe the prattling songs of the minstrels, and the well-worn legends of the people, who have not allowed the heroic deeds of the Hungarians up till now to fall into oblivion." After Arpád had conquered the land, he marched with his people into the castle of Attila, where everything was waste and neglected. "In the ruins"—says the Anonymous—"they held daily banquets, they sat in rows in the palace of Attila, and the sounds and sweet tones of their lutes and shalms, and all sorts of songs from their vocalists,echoed from the company." Along with the Anonymous notary other chroniclers also mention the numerous hymns, dirges and martial songs, the latter of which were forthcoming in great numbers, and enjoyed universal favour.

The minstrels, reciters, and jongleurs can be regarded as the makers of these songs, who already at Arpád's time sang their heroic songs at national festivities, which came into popular use thereby. The name "igricz," of slavic origin, used to refer to Harlequinades, Mummeries, and buffooneries, and since it was not in the nature of the Hungarians to take part in common antics, in frivolous buffooneries, or to feel any particular pleasure therein, it is probable that these jongleurs were of foreign nationality. In their place came the Troubadours later, whose name is by many people derived from "tréfa" (fun).

Many interesting facts about the dance of the Hungarians are found in the Chronicle of the Monk of St. Gallen, Ekkehard (10th century). He relates that in the Hungarian dance there are seven steps. He names it "Siebensprünge" ("the Seven Steps"). This dance was taught to the people of the Lake of Constance by the Hungarians during the latter's residence there, who later under the name of "Hun step" applied this dance to their own slow moving dance.

Many aver that the leaders themselves made the old Hungarian heroic songs, the minstrels being only their exponents, after having put them to music.

All testimony points to the fact that at Arpád's time music was not only beloved by great personages, but also among the people. It is known of Bishop Gerhard, that, when he came from his seat Csanád with Walther, the singing-master of the Fehérvár School, to King Stephen I., he passed the night on the way at suitable places, and through the night was awakened from his sleep by songs. The bishop turned to his conductor with the words

"Walther, do you hear how sweet the song of the Hungarians is?" Since the songs grew clearer and clearer, Gerhard continued: "Walther, tell me, what causes this song which compels me to interrupt my slumbers?" On this, Walther declared that a girl was the singer, who ground wheat on a handmill and whiled away her hard work with singing. Thus the Hungarians had already at that time a taste for singing, and carried on their hard work while singing, just as at present, when the most beautiful Hungarian folk-songs arise at ploughing and sowing, at the harvest and the vintage.

The Hungarian music must have had great repute even 800 years ago, for when the Hungarians fought as allies of the Russian prince Isislav, against the Poles and Bohemians, and, after a victorious fight, marched with triumphal pomp into Kiev, the townspeople got up festivities in honour of their guests, and "the house was fortunate in which Hungarian music sounded."

We know from descriptions that the following instruments were in use in Hungary: the Lute (koboz, a kind of Indian Lyre), and the Violin (hegedü) likewise a string-instrument. Of wind-instruments, large and small pipes were made out of willow twigs—which are still a popular instrument like the Shepherd's pipe (*tilinkó*) ;—the horn made out of the buffalo or ox's horn called "kürt"; the small hand-drum, like a Moorish tambourine, but without castanets. It is best to assume that the Hungarians brought these musical instruments from their original home. The field-trumpet and the cymbal were of later date.

With regard to form, opinions about the old lutes are various. Most probably it was like the Indian national instrument, the *Vina*. The player sat, laid it on his knee, and played *pizzicato*. Among the Székelys, in Transylvania, there is still a similar instrument which is so played and is called the "timbora."

Unfortunately we know not a single melody from the music of the Huns' songs, nor from the time of the old heathenism, but from the manner of life and the continual wars of our people it is self-evident that the music of that time must have been dramatic and heroic. The best proof of its once high development are the old Hungarian legends and traditions, which relate in song the fortunate or unfortunate careers of the nation, the heroic deeds of Attila, Arpád, and the dukes. The melodies of these songs were gradually lost in the advance of Christianity, and it is probable that, with the crushing of Vata's rebellion, very many precious poetical and musical products of the ancient days of heathen Hungary were entirely destroyed.

Under Stephen I., and later, the Christian church-music spread also among us, and the Gregorian song soon took root here, too, as among all the other proselytes to Christianity. The schools founded by Stephen I. and his successors had a two-fold task: to educate in Christian religion and in song.

In the first of these schools founded be Bishop Gregory at Székesfehérvár, the forementioned Walther instructed the children of thirty christianised families in Latin and in song.

Several bishops followed this example, and thus schools arose in Esztergom, Pannonhalma, Vácz, Veszprém, Nagyvárad and Nyitra.

The church-music had some influence on our popular songs is plain from certain Folk-songs whose melody is constructed on the Scale of Church-music, which at the same time is a convincing proof of their age. In these songs, though the words are more recent, the melodies plainly show the influence of Christian Church-music.

Since the first priests in Hungary were

strangers and principally Italians, as a matter of course they taught the young people only Latin songs. Later, when several natives became clergymen, they spread the Church-songs in Hungarian translations, composed church-songs themselves, Hymns with Hungarian text which, however, by a law of King Kálmán's time (1112) could only be adopted among Church-songs on approval by the Synod.

Our annals mention several such composers of this time, among the rest Andreas Vásárhelyi, who wrote a song to the Virgin as Patroness of Hungary, and an unknown composer, whose song on St. Stephen was printed at Nüremburg in 1454.

From this time the Hungarian text of another church song has come down to us, the Königsberg fragment "On the virginity of the Virgin Mary." The tunes of the three songs mentioned we do not know, but they cannot have been aught else than the ordinary Gregorian Hymns.

We must now mention two pre-eminent Hungarians, who have acquired European renown by their art. The first was Nicolas Klinsor in the 13th Century, a Transylvanian who lived at the court of Andreas III., and as one of the most learned of the Master Singers took part in the competition held at the Wartburg near Eisenach in 1208 at the invitation of the German Minnesinger, Henry von Ofterdingen. Some of his songs are found in the old epic poem: Der Sängerkrieg auf der Wartburg (the singing match at the Wartburg). Still more famous was George Szlatkoni (Slakoni, Slakona), born in Krajna near Nyitra, 1456, who at the beginning of the 16th century was the 4th bishop of St. Stephen's church in Vienna, and as privy councillor and choir-master to Emperor Maximilian I. distinguished himself in religious and secular music alike.*)

* Among the pictures of Hans Burgmayer (Imperial and Royal Library, Vienna) which contain

At the court of the Hungarian Kings of mixed families foreign masters often found employment. The Capellmeister of King Sigismund was the renowned Georg Stolzer, Josquin des Prés' contemporary. At the court of King Mathias, the great Netherland theorist, Johann Tinctoris, resided, who was the Capellmeister of King Ferdinand of Naples and the music-master of his daughter Beatrice. Beatrice brought him with her to Hungary, and

---

135 woodcuts and exhibit the triumph of the Emperor Maximilian, our countryman is portrayed sitting in a cant equipage and directing his band of singers and musicians. Under the picture is the word "Apollo." The explanation appended to the pictures thus alludes to Szlakoni:

Szlakoni (Bishop in Vienna) is to be made Capellmeister, and the rhyme has reference to the fact, that, by direction of the Emperor, he arranged the singing of the choir in a most charming manner:

In consonance and harmony,
In melody and symphony,
In every art to my desire
Have I improved the tuneful choir.
And yet the honour not to me
But to my Emperor must be.

under him the court-band and the singers of King Matthias attained world-wide renown. According to Peter, Bishop of Vulturan and legate of Sixtus IV., there was no better choir at that time than that of King Matthias.

This fact plainly shows that King Matthias fostered music, and that the Queen as well as he had a band and a choir. In addition there was a well-organized band of trumpets. The band of the King and Queen must have consisted of 30 executants, which was reckoned an extraordinary number for that time, if we compare the Vienna band of Leopold some centuries later, which was only 18 strong.

Tinctoris dedicated to Queen Beatrice one of his renowned theoretical works. At the same time lived Monetarius, born at Selmecz, who distinguished himself as a composer and by a theoretical work, which he dedicated to George Thurzó in 1513.

Even King Wladislaus II., renowned for his great poverty, spent 200 pieces of gold yearly on his singers and musicians.

Under Lewis II. Adrian Willaert, of Netherland birth (afterwards the founder of the Venetian School), lived seven years at Buda, and left Hungary after the battle of Mohács. Willaert, the creator of the Madrigal, dedicated to the wife of Lewis II. a madrigal consisting of several parts, which is preserved in St. Mark's Library at Venice.

The residence of these illustrious personages in our land, who were all disciples of the old counterpoint, has exercised small influence on the character of the Hungarian music, for singers and instruments alike were brought sometimes out of Italy, sometimes from Germany, and, while they figured as court musicians only in churches and at court festivities, Hungarian music drew little advantage from their sojourn here and only a few popular songs have descended to us, e.g., the song "Mátyást mostan választotta" (King Matthias has been elected) which the children sang at Matthias' election to the throne.

In King Sigismund's time there were organs in many churches. There is a well known document of John Hunyadi (1452) in which the parish of Felsö-Bánya is allowed certain expenses for the erection of an organ. The first introduction of this instrument, however, cannot be historically indicated. According to Nicolas Oláh an organ with silver pipes was played at Visegrád in the chapel of King Matthias, whereas at Buda Masses with song were celebrated; thus not only was the royal Cathedral (Matthias' church) decorated with an organ, but there was also instrumental music corresponding to the time.

With regard to the Hungarian Folksongs and Dance Music, no certain data have come down to us from these centuries: * still we may assume that it went on

* The 10th to the 15th centuries.

a way of its own despite foreign influence. Conspicuous executants of Hungarian dance-music were the wandering gipsies of the 14th century, and they especially spread the Hungarian secular instrumental music. Not only the people patronized them, but they were willingly entertained at the courts of the magnates. They played a rôle not only in festivities, but sometimes also at the Parliament meetings, of which our historians make mention, at the noisy assemblies at Rákos and Hatvan in 1525. The most conspicuous was Dominik Kármán who, according to Tinódi, enjoyed great renown as a lutist and a violinist. A verse of Tinódi testifies that the lute at that time was played by the fingers, but the violin was already played by the gipsies with the bow.

In the 18th century Michael Barna and Czinka Panna, distinguished themselves—the former being called the Hungarian Orpheus—on whose life and death numerous Latin poems were written. Johann Bihary followed them, one of the most illustrious, whose recruiting tunes and *Primate*, *Palatine*, and *Coronation* tunes are among the most beautiful of Hungarian dances. He and his band were invited more than once to the Court-balls at Vienna. He gave concerts in Hungary, Transylvania, Poland, and Vienna; the great Beethoven listened to his playing often with great pleasure, and has used the melody of a slow Hungarian tune of Bihary's in his overture dedicated to King Stephen. At present our gipsy bands win laurels not only in Europe but also in America and Asia, reaping both money and renown. They deserve our thanks for spreading Hungarian music.

Returning to earlier centuries, we must not forget war-songs and camp-music. History mentions as composers of this style John Cesinge, who, as Bishop of Pécs (15th century), placed himself at the head of his troops, and inspired his soldiers to battle by his songs. Several Hungarian lutists had repute in Europe already in the 16th century. One was Valentine Bakfark, others say Graevisius (born in Transylvania 1507, died at Padua 1576), who lived chiefly in Poland. He came at the invitation of the emperor Maximilian to Vienna (1570) where he played a rôle at court. He lived long at the court of the Polish King August Sigismund, with whom he must have been on intimate terms, at least the preface of one of his works says as much. Two of his works have come down to us: Premier livre de tabulature de lutte (Paris, 1564), and Bakfarci Valentini Greffi Pannonii Harmoniarum musicarum usum testudinis factorum (Cracoviæ, 1566). He dedicated the last work to the Polish King, who bestowed on him a property as leader of the court band. John Bakfark—probably son of the foregoing—was also a lute virtuoso of great fame. Among the works of both we find several compositions written in Hungarian style.

As excellent lutist must be named John Newsidler, who was born in Pozsony. His school for the Lute appeared in Nuremberg. In the first volume of this work he treats of Lute tablature. In the second volume are several Fantasias, Preludes, Psalms and Motetts.

A contemporary of his was Christopher Armpruster, also born in Transylvania, whose Pamphlet, "Song on morality," appeared in print in 1551.

In the 16th century are conspicuous Andreas Batizi (1546) with his "Fair history of the Holy Marriage of the Patriarch Isaac," Andreas Farkas (1538) with "How God led Israel's people from Egypt and similarly the Hungarians from Scythia," Peter Kákonyi, Peter Désy, Kasper Bajnai, Stephan Csükei, Michael Sztáray, Blasius Székely, and Michael Tarjay, who have also written songs with biblical purport, and whose style despite their religious character, is quite Hungarian. In the airs there is much melodious invention. Many a song sounds just like an earnest slow Hungarian tune. We see, therefore, how, even in the 16th century, those who were of pure Hungarian race were concerned with music and aimed at elevating our national music not only in secular songs, but by applying it to religious ditties.

At this time Sebastian Tinódi lived, the lute-player of the 16th century, whom the people named "Sebök-deák." He was the prototype of the true lutist, wandering through the country, and playing his lute here and there. He wrote music to his songs. He was not only a true chronicler in his historical songs of the events of the 16th century, but he was the first Hungarian composer; for the musical invention of his songs and their construction are of quite a Hungarian character, and some of his songs, *e.g.* "Sok csudák" (Many a miracle),

"Siess keresztyén" (Hasten Christian) are quite unique and possess abiding worth. The tune of his song "Enyingi Török" Francis Erkel has adapted in his famous funeral march in his opera "Ladislaus Hunyadi."

Tinódi's songs passed from mouth to mouth at that time, and people began afterwards to perpetuate their style, as the numerous songs and ballads of the Thököly and Rákóczy period show.

The bloom of Hungarian music, however, began to take greater dimensions already with the spread of the Hungarian Reformation. Then the people sang in churches in their own language, and made their musical forms out of the tunes in the Psalter. At that time secular poems were often sung to the music of sacred songs, and in many tunes composed in the 17th century we recognise the tunes of the hymns of the Huguenots composed by Gaudimel which were naturalized with us.

The most brilliant period of our Folk-songs is in the time of Thököly and still more in that of Rákóczy. We can only wonder at the beauty, impressiveness, natural strength and characteristic rhythm of the so-called *Kurutz songs* and be amazed at their variety.

The Kurutz songs and other musical creations of that time are not only genuine musical pearls, but accurately reflect, also, the character and peculiarity of the Hungarian music and form the source from which the later songs, tunes, recruiting songs, wedding and other dances, and the whole body of the so-called "hallgató magyar" melodies have sprung. If we take into consideration that the great masters, Handel and Sebastian Bach, were born, or in their childhood, when these songs arose, and that Haydn, Mozart, Beethoven—this triad of geniuses—lived 50 or 60 years later, we can scarcely express our marvel at the astonishing variety and versatility of the bold forms and richness of the rhythm which had revealed itself in Hungarian music at the end of the 17th and the beginning of the 18th century. F. Liszt rightly remarks: "There is no other music from which European musicians can learn so much rhythmic originality as the Hungarian."

At this time arose "Rákóczi Ferencz dala" (Song of Francis Rákóczi), "Rákóczi siralma" (Rákóczi's complaint), and the "Rákóczi nóta" (Rákóczi Tune), from which the world-renowned Rákóczi March sprang a hundred years later.

At this period were composed the numerous melancholy songs of the exiles: "Oszi harmat" (Autumnal dew), "Ne búsulj" (Don't be grieved), "Adam Balogh's tune" and "Bercsényi's tune" which have enduring value, and also many folk-songs which arose later can be referred to this period, viz., "Repülj fecském" (Fly, my swallow), "Az ég alatt" (Under the heaven), "Vörös bársony süvegem" (My cap of red velvet),

"Zöld asztalon ég a gyertya" (The candle is burning on the green table); and many other famous songs date from the Rákóczi period.

From the middle of the 17th to the end of the 18th century, only the Song and the Tune (nóta) were known in Hungarian music. The Song was a simple Folk-song, a war-song or a hymn. By "Tune" was implied a piece of music of greater extent. There was already, as we said, Thököli, Rákóczi, Bercsényi Tunes, from which sprang later the so-called "hallgató magyar," melodies which were intended for public performance. Also the different styles of Hungarian Dance-music arose in this period.

We had two sorts of dances, Court dances and Peasant dances. The "Palace dance" and the "Slow Hungarian" were court dances, the "Dance tune" and the "Dumping tune" were Peasant dances. The old Palace Dance was known exclusively as a court dance in the 15th century.

Its music is quite different from the difficult tempoed music of its time, and from the later foreign dances: Saraband, Pavan and Minuet. Its melody was livelier and moved in quicker rhythms. The nobility and their ladies danced it; and since it only consisted of slow turns and was rather a walking dance, old ladies and gentlemen, nay, even ecclesiastics, took part in it. In the music of this dance young Knights often showed their cleverness in a Hungarian solo, but at such occasions they moved more rapidly. This dance was danced also abroad as the "Passo mezzo ongarese" or "Passo mezzo ongaro" and formed a separate part of the Italian "Ballo."

From the Palace and the Slow Hungarian Dance rose the "Verbunkos," which was danced at recruiting. No other nation beside the Hungarian possesses such a dance. Popular dances were also the *Lakodalmas* (Wedding-dance), *Incselkedö* (the "Coquettish"),

Kalákás, which were in use at weddings; the *Sátoros* (Dance of the tents), *Fegyveres* (Dance of the arms), and *Dóbogó* (Drumming-dance), which were danced in camps and after the battle.

During the forties of the 19th Century several Hungarian Society dances arose, *e.g.*, the *Körmagyar* (Ronde-magyar), the *Füzér-táncz* (Wreaths-dance), and the *Csárdás* (Tavern-dance), which is still in vogue.

As an excellent dance-composer, John Latova must be mentioned, belonging to the last century, who has written more than 80 works of this class. Antonis Csermák and Markus Rózsavölgyi who has written many excellent dances, followed him.

At the end of the 17th century some of our artists attained celebrity and brought honour to Hungary abroad. One of these was J. Sigismund Cousser, born at Pozsony, who in 1697 at Hamburg helped Mattheson and Kaiser to create the first

German opera. He produced a large number of his operas there. His operas Erindo (1693), Porus (1694), Pyramus and Thisbe (1694), Scipio in Africa (1697), enjoyed great favour. In 1700 he was choirmaster at Dublin Cathedral, where he died about 1730.*

In the sphere of church-music Johann Francisci, born at Beszterczebánya in 1691, attained great honour as an excellent organist. He travelled through Germany, knew Mattheson and J. S. Bach, and had such renown that one of his friends in Breslau, Joh. Glettinger (1725), was inspired to make the following panegyric:

> Illustrious friend, Amphion's progeny;
> My fancy finds art's true ideal in thee.

---

* The following works appeared in print:— "Apollon enjoué," containing six overtures, "The joy of the Muses" (Nüremberg, 1700), "Ode on the death after renouned Arabella Hunt" (London), "Serenade on the Birthday of the English King, George I.," Dublin (1724).

Thy songs are like an angel's songs above,
And thus the world bestows on thee her love;
This only wish have I at my command,
That thou may'st be the Orpheus of thy land.

In 1733 he was invited to Pozsony, where he lived as church-choirmaster. He returned to his native land to a similar post in 1735.

In the second half of the preceding century the higher circles cultivated secular music, especially Italian and German, to a great degree. They kept excellent bands, and invited to their conductorship illustrious foreign conductors.

The Esterházys' were pre-eminent for their patronage of music. Duke Nicholas Esterházy, and afterwards his son Paul, had in Kis-Marton a theatre erected with great luxury, and a distinguished band, at the head of which was Joseph Haydn, afterwards Ignatz Pleyel, and lastly Johann Nep. Hummel. The Károlyis had permanent bands and theatres in Megyer, the Batthyany's in Rohoncz, and the

Erdödy's in Pozsony. The higher clergy were not behindhand in the culture of music and kept in their residences singers and musicians, placing distinguished foreign masters at their head, which was of great influence to the formation of the Church style and also of secular music. The illustrious contrapuntist and theorist Albrechtsberger, Beethoven's master, lived at Györ, Michael Haydn also and Karl Dittersdorf in Nagy-Várad. They all exercised great influence on the development of the musical life in the towns mentioned. That influence can still be seen in all the towns where there was a standing band, for at these places the taste for music and its encouragement has remained among the people till the present day. As examples. let us quote Kassa, Eger, Nagy-Várad, Pécs, Pozsony, Temesvár, where an excellent soil is prepared not only for concerts, but for theatrical exhibitions. After many of these bandmasters, musicians and singers had founded families and remained in our land, the cultivation of music came more into fashion. Piano-playing began to spread at the beginning of this century. There was scarcely a nobleman's house, where this instrument was not found. For this reason several illustrious foreign masters settled in Hungary and occupied themselves with pianoforte teaching. These masters were disciples of Haydn, Mozart, Beethoven, and thus the piano compositions of these three geniuses were introduced into aristocratic circles, where there must have been excellent players, since Beethoven has dedicated several of his classical piano sonatas to Hungarian ladies of high rank. The taste for music soon spread in middle-class society, and from this class proceeded our best musicians and composers. We must thank this movement for the fact that several Hungarian instruction-books appeared at the beginning of the century. The first School for

Piano was written by Stephen Gati (Buda 1809), which was followed by Dömény's and Milovitzkys Piano School, and a course of Harmony entitled the "Hungarian Apollo" by Andreas Bartay.

All these publications had a favourable effect on the development of music in general and that of Hungarian music in particular.

The number of those who cultivated Hungarian music was already considerable.

From their ranks Johann Fuss arose (born Tolna, 1777, died Vienna, 1819) who was so conspicuous as a composer of all styles of music that he awoke the interest of Haydn. He generally lived at Vienna, but in 1800 he was invited to Pozsony as composer, where he received universal esteem. He wrote string quartettes, trios, duos for violin and piano, sonatas for piano, solos and duets, overtures, sacred works and numerous duologues. The greater part of his works are printed.

Two countrymen of ours attained world-wide renown at the beginning of this century—Johann Nep. Hummel (born on Nov. 14th, 1778, at Pozsony), and Franz Liszt (born 22nd October, 1811, at the village of Doborján, in the County of Sopron). Hummel as a pianist belonged to the last cultivation of the classical style, and excelled by his free improvisa-ion. The number of his compositions exceeds 120, of which his concertos for the piano and his renowned Septet for Wind instruments are of abiding worth. He died at Weimar on the 7th of October, 1837. His birth place, Pozsony, erected a statue to his memory in 1888.

Franz Liszt, awoke such wonder by his piano-playing in his 9th year, that he was called the second Mozart. The families of Szapâry, Apponyi, Esterházy, and Erdödy guaranteed a yearly amount for the child's education. His father took him to Vienna, where Charles Czerny and Salieri were his masters. At this time he was introduced to Beethoven who prophesied a brilliant future for the boy, and kissed him publicly at his first concert at Vienna. At the age of 16—17 he ravished the world with his concerts. At the end of 1848 he abandoned the rôle of virtuoso, devoted himself to composition and settled in Weimar. There he began to write his incomparable Hungarian Rhapsodies, 15 in all, in which he employed the prettiest Folk-songs, and Dances, and the Rákóczy March. By his means Hungarian music was spread and made popular in Europe. He was the creator of the Rhapsody and of the Symphonic Poem. In the last named composition he employed many Hungarian tunes *e.g.* in "Battle of the Huns" and "Hungaria," and proved hereby that Hungarian music is capable of being applied to serious purposes.

We should have to write books in order to do justice to his many-sidedness as a composer and to his compositions.

Also as a tone-poet he occupies a high place. He was the apostle of Richard Wagner, who later became his son-in-law, and he paved the way for that great musical reformer.

In 1862, he went to Rome, where he lived in the seclusion of the Convent Monte Maria and there under the title of an Abbé received the lowest clerical ordination. At this time he wrote his most important works, his oratorio, "St. Elizabeth," first performed in Budapest in 1865, his renowned Hungarian Coronation March in 1867 and his oratorio, "Christus," which was first performed in Budapest in 1875. In both of the former he employed many Hungarian melodies.

He was President of the Royal Hungarian Academy of Music in 1875, where he taught the piano to the highest class. He died at Bayreuth on the 31st of July, 1886.

We Hungarians may be proud of the fact that the great gladiators of piano-playing, Hummel and Liszt, were our countrymen.

A worthy contemporary of Liszt's was Francis Erkel (born 5th November, 1810, at Békés-Gyula. Died at Budapest 15th June, 1860). He can be confidently named as the creator of the Hungarian original opera, for all that was produced in this sphere before him by Joseph Rusicska with his "Flight of Béla," Joseph Heinisch with his "Election of King Matthias," and Andreas Bartay with his opera entitled "Cunning," can scarcely be regarded as aught else than as a more or less successful attempt at soaring, although genuine Hungarian music played a considerable part in these works. Francis Erkel's merits on this field are immortal. He showed the path to be followed and the means to be adopted that Hungarian opera might be a worthy companion of foreign musical drama. In 1848 he wrote "Maria Báthori," this was followed by "Ladislaus Hunyadi," which was received with enthusiasm. Individual parts of this opera, the remarkable overture, the swan song, the church scene, the funeral March, can be said to be of classical value in the literature of Hungarian music. In 1860 his "Bánk Bán" was performed. In this work he attained very original and striking effects by the use of the Hungarian cymbal, along with old instruments seldom employed. In the scene on the banks of the Tisza he made the shepherd's pipe sound (of course represented by 2 piccolos) and gives to individual scenes a thoroughly Hungarian character. His opera "Sarolta" was performed in 1862. "George Dóza" followed in 1874, "Nameless Heroes" in 1880, "George Brankovics" in 1874 and "King Stephen" in 1885. The last work he wrote in his 76th year, despite which the melodic invention and instrumentation are as fresh as in his [early ?] works.

He also takes first place as bandmaster.

In his artistic life of more than half a century he laid the foundations of the Philharmonic Concerts in Budapest, in 1850, and conducted them for eighteen years.

We cannot speak with detail of his services as bandmaster but can only mention the fact that it is through him that the orchestra of the National Theatre has gained European renown. His name will always live as the composer of the national hymn "Isten âldd meg a magyart" (God save the Magyar) so long as there is a Hungarian in the land.

As a dramatic composer Charles Goldmark stands in the first rank, who, in the sphere of symphonies, chamber music, and song composition, enjoys a wide reputation not only in his own country but in all the cultivated world. Goldmark was born at Keszthely in 1832. He awoke real enthusiasm in 1860 when he came before the public with his Suite composed for violin and piano and his

Overture " Sakuntala " of eastern character. Goldmark belongs to those preeminent men of talent who distinguish themselves by originality, feeling, a vein of poetry, noble inspiration and interesting harmony. He is also a master of brilliant orchestration. Of his works the most remarkable are the Symphony "The Country Wedding," the overtures "Penthesilea," "Spring," and "Sappho." These works are found in the repertoires of Philharmonic Concerts all the world over. He gained the greatest success with his opera, "The Queen of Sheba" (1873). In this work his musical talents are at their best. In 1886, thirteen years later, his opera "Merlin" was performed. In this he abandoned his eastern style, and, curbing his individuality, has produced a work of grand style and of noble melody, which is almost equal to the "Queen of Sheba." Of late he has tried his powers in the lyric sphere, and with his new opera "A házi tücsök" (Cricket on the hearth) he has repeatedly shown his many-sided brilliant talents. His music has much of Hungarian character in melody and conception alike.

Goldmark works slowly and re-writes much, but what he does write, be it a piece for the piano, a song, an orchestral piece, or an opera, all stands on a high level.

In the sphere of opera there are at present Karl Thern, the composer of Vörösmarty's "Song of Fót," whose operas "Gizul" and "The Siege of Tihany," gained great success in 1840; further, Charles Huber with his comic opera, "The Székely Maid," into which he has worked several of our prettiest songs. Charles Huber has done much as a violin teacher; he wrote an excellent violin school into the practical part of which he has incorporated many Hungarian songs. From his compositions we must single out "5 Hungarian Fantasias for Violin and Piano," and many patriotic male choruses,

"Freedom's song," "Memory of our Ancestors," "National flags," "For holy fatherland," "Song of inspiration," etc.

His son Eugene Hubay is one of the most renowned violinists, who enjoys great fame not only in Hungary but abroad. Thus far he has written three operas. "Alienor," and "The Lutanist of Cremona," were first performed in the Royal Hungarian Opera House. With the latter he gained success abroad. Of late he has struck out a new style with his opera "Falu rossza" (The bad fellow of the village)—the so-called popular operetta, which from beginning to end contains the prettiest Hungarian music, while the new arts of modern technique are applied simultaneously.

A very cultivated, fertile, and many-sided man is Edmund Mihalovich. As a composer he is a disciple of the new school. The style of the Symphonic Poem, created by Liszt, he cultivates with success. His works, "Hero and Leander," "La

Ronde du Sabbat," "The ghostly vessel," and "Sellö" (Nymph) are all eminent. His tunes are noble, his orchestration masterly. Thus far he has written two operas, "Hagbarth und Signe" and "Toldi's Love." In Hungarian music he is very successful, as is proved by his compositions for orchestra, "Dirge in memory of Francis Deâk," and "Toldi's Love." Richard Wagner highly esteemed his musical talents, and wrote "Wieland the Smith" for him. Francis Sârossy has also written the successful operas "Atala" and "The last Abencerage."

It is a matter for congratulation that we have talented composers among the younger generation. One of these is Emerich Elbert, who has shown dramatic power in the opera "Tamora"; further Edmund Farkas whose two operas, "The Penitents" and "Valentin Balassa," are written with beautiful melodic invention; Julius Mannheimer whose opera "Maritana," and Maurice Varinecz whose "Rosamunda" and "Ratclif" have been performed abroad.

As cultivators of Hungarian music we must mention Michael Mosonyi (born in 1814 in Boldogasszonyfalva, county Moson), and Cornelius Abrányi, sen., who have rendered great services in the development of Hungarian music. Mosonyi in the fifties played a leading rôle in Pesth, and was an authority on church and chamber music. He wrote string quartets, Symphonies and religious compositions. In 1850 he applied himself with all his heart to the cultivation of Hungarian music. He gained great success with his pièces de circonstance: The memory of Kazinczy, Széchényi-Mourning, Festive Ouverture, Victory and Grief of the Hungarian Honvéd. The Hungarian ballad, the song, the male and mixed choruses, the Cantata and the opera are beholden to him for excellent works. Among his best works are "The Festival of the old Hungarians at the river Ung" and "Fair Ilona," a romantic Hungarian opera.

As teacher and distinguished musical savant he had excellent scholars, *e.g.*, Alexander Erkel, Julius Erkel, Edmund Mihalovich, Ladislaus Zimay, etc. He died in 1870. Franz Liszt composed a funeral March in his memory.

Cornelius Abrányi played not only an important rôle in the spread of Hungarian music, but as composer he also takes a high place. His songs and ballads for solo voice, his fantasias for piano, are excellent specimens of Hungarian music. He has distinguished himself also as a writer on music. He founded the first Hungarian musical journal. He wrote instruction books, such as A School of Composition, A General History of Music and The Peculiarities of Hungarian Music. He founded at Arad the National Choral Society. The number of his compositions reaches nearly 100.

Edward Bartay has done much for the spread of Hungarian Music. From 1860 he has taken an active part in our musical movements. At present he is director of the National Conservatorium. He has written piano pieces, choruses, and instrumental works, which have been often performed with success. In the cultivation of orchestral and chamber music Julius Beliczay, I. Julius Major, Francis Xav. Szabó, Paul Jámbor, Arpád Késmárky and Isidor Bátor are eminent for many excellent works.

Virtuoso playing which Liszt brought to great perfection has had great exponents also in our country, among them Emerik Székely (born in 1823 at Mátyusfalva, county Ugocsa) must be mentioned. Among his compositions are string quartets, trios and sonatas, but his fame is founded on his 32 Hungarian Fantasias, written for piano, and his 12 music idylls in which he has elaborated the greates treasures of our modern Folk-songs.

Stephen Heller, the illustrious pianist, born at Budapest in 1815, achieved great success in 1830. The number of his works for the piano is 140. They are characterised by originality, good taste, elegant treatment and richness of melody. Since 1838 he lived at Paris, where he took first rank among distinguished pianoforte teachers, and where he died.*

A Hungarian pianist of European renown is Count Géza Zichy, who, in his 14th year, by an unlucky wound from a gun lost his right arm. By unwearied diligence he succeeded in training his left hand so that not only in Hungary but in the whole cultivated world he had excited the greatest admiration by his pianoforte playing. As a composer he has written several songs, many excellent works for choruses and the opera "Alar." He

---

* Stephen Heller, although born at Budapest, was not, however, an Hungarian. His parents were German Jews who had settled in Pesth. ED. MUSICAL STANDARD.

writes almost all the text to his own compositions.

In the composition of Hungarian songs, ballads, and male choruses the principal writers are: Benjamin Egressy the author of the melody of the "Szózat," with his noble popular songs; Ladislaus Zimay, Victor Langer, Ernest Lányi, with their romances; Alexander Erkel, the distinguished bandmaster, with his patriotic male choruses; Francis Gaál and Alois Tarnay. With our musical literature there is closely connected a species of Hungarian drama, the Popular Play, which takes its subjects from common life and which has the Folk-song and the dance as one of its principal elements. Edward Szigligety was the creator of this style of art. To his first two pieces, "Szökött Katona" (The Deserter), and "Csikós" (The Coltherd), Josef Szerdahelyi wrote the music, using for that purpose our oldest and most original songs. Also the music to "Matyás Diák" (The student Matthias), Bányarém" (The terror of the mine), "Liliomfi" is written by him. Later writers of the same order are Benjamin Egressy, Ignaz Bognár, Julius Káldy, Julius Erkel, Alexander Nikolits. Executants in this branch are Mimi de Cau, Michel Füredy, Josef Tamásy, Madame Hegedüs, and Madame Blaha. This style of drama greatly contributed to the fact that popular Hungarian music became known and appreciated abroad, for our publishers, directly after the performance of a piece, published the prettiest songs in it and circulated them not only in Hungary but also in Europe, so as to admit of foreign composers familiarising themselves with Hungarian music.

We should have to write a regular anthology if we reckoned up all the compositions which famous foreign composers have written in the Hungarian style, or in which they have used Hungarian songs. In the works of Haydn, Beethoven, Schubert, and Weber we find many Hungarian passages. We can mention only a few of the later composers, and thus we may credit Berlioz with the transcription of the renowned Rákôczy march; Volkmann with "Visegrâd," Twelve sketches for piano called "Hungarian sketches," "Souvenir of Maroth;" "At the tomb Count Széchényi;" John Brahms with four volumes of Hungarian dances, Hungarian and Gipsy songs; Raff with Hungarian dances; Hofmann with a Hungarian suite; Bülow a "Heroic March;" Massenet, Hungarian March; Delibes, parts of his ballet "Copélia;" Mascagni, "Friend Fritz." Besides these the famous pianoforte and violin artists Dreischock, Thalberg, Wilmers, Schulhof, Rubinstein, Molique, Sarasate have written for their instruments Variations and Fantasias in Hungarian style with the introduction of favourite songs. When in 1860 operettas came into fashion some composers tried their powers in this branch. Among the earlier ones were

Géza Allaga and Charles Huber; afterwards Julius Káldy, Alexius Erkel, Béla Hegyi, Eugene Stojanovitcs.

More recently some have gained success in ballet music, and excellent music has been written by Charles Szabados, who with his ballet, "Viora," roused great enthusiasm. Eugene Stojanovitcs with his ballet "Csárdás," Stephen Kerner with "Le cheval de bronze," Lewis Tóth and Albert Metz with their ballet "Day and Night," have shown excellent powers of composition.

Many conspicuous countrymen of ours have won honour for Hungary abroad, *e.g.*, Josef Joachim, the greatest violinist of modern times, the Director of the High School in Berlin. Also among his compositions the most valuable is the Hungarian Concerto. Edward Reményi, Leopold Auer, Director of the Conservatorium at St. Petersburg, Edmund Singer, Rafael Josephi. Renowned conductors are Hans Richter, Sucher (Berlin), Seidel

(New York); singers: Mme. Mainville, Mme. Schoedel, Louise Liebhardt, Cornelia Hollósy, Rosa Csillag, Ida Benza, Francis Steger, Josef Wurda, John Beck, Lewis Bignio, etc.

As pianists and teachers we must further mention Antonio Sipos, with his numerous compositions for the piano, John Theindl and Willy Deutsch, who took an active part in the musical life of the capital. Teachers of composition were Michael Mosonyi and Alexander Nikolits; one might almost say that nearly all the younger generation have had their education from them. As writers on music beside the above mentioned Abrányi, are Gabriel Mátray and Stephen Bartalus. The first made the old Hungarian music known by his work "The melodies of historical, biblical and satirical Hungarian songs of the 17th century." Bartalus issued his interesting publication, "The Hungarian Orpheus," a collection of miscellaneous matter of the 18th and 19th centuries and a general collection of Hungarian songs.

Recently Julius Kâldy with his works, "The Treasures of old Hungarian Music," "Old Hungarian War Songs," "Recruiting Songs," "Songs and Marches of the War for Freedom," has aroused much enthusiasm.

We must mention that in Hungary since the beginning of this century many institutions and schools for the cultivation of music have arisen. In Kolozsvár in 1819, the first Hungarian Conservatorium now existing was founded (the first Hungarian Opera was performed there in 1821). In 1833 Arad followed this example. An artistic association founded a similar institution at Pesth called The Musicians Society, which in its turn founded the National Conservatoire. In 1860, Debreczen founded in its turn a Conservatoire, while Kassa, Szeged and Sabadka, followed its example.

In 1860 the National Dramatic School

was opened in Budapest, in which operatic song was also taught. At the same time the Society of Musical Amateurs was founded, and the Musical Academy of Buda. Later in both these institutes a Music School was organized. In 1875 the National Hungarian Academy of Music was opened with Franz Liszt and Francis Erkel at the head of it. Ultimately the Hungarian School of Music was opened under the presidency of Julius Káldy, Alexander Nikolits and Julius Major, who have undertaken the special field of cultivation and instruction in Hungarian music.

Beside these there are in Budapest, as in the larger provincial towns, many musical and choral societies, and at Budapest as brilliant a concert season as at Vienna or Leipzig. In the first rank we must name the concerts of the Philharmonic Society, the Budapest Society of amateurs, the Buda Musical Academy, also the performances of the National

Academy of Music, the National and the Hungarian School of Music, and also the concerts of the several musical societies. We must add the appearance of many famous foreign violinists, pianists and singers who visit Budapest regularly.

Lately historical concerts have been started, by Stephen Bartalus and Julius Káldy reviving the most precious relics of the 17th and 18th centuries. These concerts, in consequence of their historical and scientific character, are generally given in the Hungarian Academy of Sciences.

We have cause for pride that Hungarian music has in a comparatively short time reached so high a level. If we compare it with the music of other nations the Italian, French, and German, the result is really surprising. At the Festivities of the thousandth year of the nation we can point to world-renowned composers among our countrymen and eminent works in all branches of music, and having regard to the past development and advance of Hungarian music we can look with full confidence and with great hope to the future.

REEVES'

MUSICAL LITERATURE LIST

BIOGRAPHY
HISTORY
CRITICISM
ÆSTHETICS
ESSAYS

ORGAN
ORCHESTRA
PIANO
VIOLIN
VOCAL

GENERAL
ETC

CONTAINING WORKS

In All Departments of . .

. . . . Musical Literature

PUBLISHED BY

W. REEVES, 83, Charing Cross Rd., London, W.C.

Revised Editions of this Catalogue B are issued in the Spring and Autumn of each year.

List of New Books to be issued in the Autumn of 1910.

THE FUTURE OF MUSIC. Coming Changes Outlined in Regard to Composer, Conductor and Orchestra. By LOUIS LALOY. Author of "Aristoxene et la Musique de l'Antiquité," "Claude Debussy," "Rameau," "La Musique Chinoise." Translated by MRS. FRANZ LIEBICH. 8vo, paper cover, 1s. net.

MODERN TENDENCIES AND OLD STANDARDS IN MUSICAL ART. By J. ALFRED JOHNSTONE, *Hon. L.Mus T.C.L.* Author of "Touch, Phrasing and Interpretation," "The Art of Teaching Piano Playing," etc. Crown 8vo, cloth.

WELL-KNOWN PIANO SOLOS. How to Play them with Understanding, Expression and Effect. By C. W. WILKINSON. Third Series. 1s.

SOME MUSICAL RECOLLECTIONS OF FIFTY YEARS. By RICHARD HOFFMAN. With Memoir by MRS. HOFFMAN. Illustrated with many Plate Portraits. Crown 8vo, cloth, 6s. 1910

Delightful reminiscences of musicians and musical affairs in America and England. The account of Mendelssohn's leading of the "Elijah" at Manchester; of Jenny Lind and her appearance at Castle Garden and her tour of America under P. T. Barnum; of Thalberg. Von Bulow, Gottschalk Liszt, and many others, and of the audiences and concerts throughout the country fifty years ago, makes most interesting reading.

VOICE PRODUCTION. A Series of Three Lectures. With Diagrams and Illustrations. By REV. CHARLES GIB.

ON THE MODAL ACCOMPANIMENT OF PLAIN CHANT. A Practical Treatise. By EDWIN EVANS, *Senior, F.R.C.O.* Author of "Technics of the Organ," "Handbook to the Works of Brahms," "How to Compose Within the Lyric Form," "The Relation of Tchaïkovsky to Art Questions of the Day," "How to Accompany at the Piano," etc.

MUSIC DURING THE VICTORIAN ERA. Being the Memoirs of J. W. Davison, Forty Years Musical Critic of "The Times." By his Son, HENRY DAVISON. With numerous Portraits and Facsimiles. Thick 8vo, cloth.

(Continued on page 48.)

IMAGINARY INTERVIEWS WITH GREAT COMPOSERS.

A Series of Vivid Pen Sketches in which the Salient Characteristics and the often Extravagant Individuality of each Composer are Truthfully Portrayed. By GERALD CUMBERLAND Crown 8vo, cloth, gilt top, 6s.

"They are vivid impressionist sketches, cleverly executed, and very interesting."—*Music.*

RUTLAND BOUGHTON, in the columns of *The Musical Standard* writes: "These are not mere fantastic juggleries, but studies of the various composers from their own standpoints to their art. They afford, with one or two striking exceptions a really valuable insight into the very nature of the different masters; and so into the nature of their music. And because of this the book will be a great help to the musical student. When we are set to study music we are generally crammed to choking-point with theoretical and anatomical instruction; and because that deals only with the appearance of the art, it is of very little final value. But a book like this of Cumberland's cuts right to the core of the composer's heart and so opens up for us a direct way to the innermost secrets of his mood and emotion . . . . . The Beethoven interview is large and dark and fierce and tender. A reading of it will give a better introduction to the Fifth and Ninth Symphonies and the greatest sonatas, than a year's course of analytical study . . . a book which is musical criticism in the highest and only final sense of the word. A book of sympathetic interpretation is constructive work. A book of analytical theory is nihilism. The publisher may congratulate himself on his share of the production, it is one of the best things he has done."

"There may be people who will read Mr. Cumberland's book simply as literature, not so much for what he says as for the way he says it. Mr. Cumberland has a wealth of expression and a delicacy and a balance that keep it ever in check. Whether he visits the femininely fanciful Chopin, the primly genial Haydn, the sombre sensitive Tchaikovsky or the gay, yet business-like, Arthur Sullivan, he knows how to draw out his man . . . . Each of his interviews is the revelation of a personality and each is a masterly piece of literary presentment . . . . Mr. Cumberland has put musicians under a debt of gratitude by placing in their hands a book that will do more than inform, that will inspire."—PERCY A. SCHOLES in *Musical Opinion.*

"To conjure up visions of the creator of a wonderful symphony or a great choral work in his surroundings, and to picture the various influences that are making their indelible mark on his manuscript; what can prompt a wider understanding, a keener appreciation and a sounder criticism of the finished score? . . . . Biographies of academic severity and critical analysis fill our library shelves, but little or nothing has been written calculated to enlist or stimulate a greater interest in the psychological thought and instincts of the great musical geniuses. The outlook of a philosopher is often the subject of a dozen critical and discursive publications. Yet the equally important consideration of the peculiar pedantries of the individual composer, as treated in these imaginary interviews, seems wholly original . . . . The book should be read by all music-lovers."—*Manchester City News.*

"All lovers of music will delight in the perusal of this extremely readable volume . . . . the reader will learn much of that psychological complexity that often accompanies great and creative genius. Although the interviews are but sketches they contain nothing that is not essentially true and characteristic."—*Montrose Standard.*

THE FUTURE OF MUSIC, Coming Changes Outlined in Regard to Composer, Conductor and Orchestra. By LOUIS LALOY. Author of "Aristoxene et la Musique de l'Antiquité," "Claude Debussy," "Rameau," "La Musique Chinoise." Translated by MRS. FRANZ LIEBICH. 8vo, paper cover, 1s. net.

504 **OLD WELSH AIRS.** The Lays of My-Land. Alawon Fy Ngwlad. Collected by N. BENNETT. Arranged for the Pianoforte or Harp by D. E. EVANS. With 12 Portraits of the old Welsh Harpers, and a short Account of their Lives. Together with an Essay on Pennilion Singing. Portraits of 10 Celebrated Pennilion Singers. 198 pages, the original two volumes bound in one vol., folio, cloth gilt, lettered 12s. 6d. net.

The above is the largest collection of Welsh Airs ever published and includes some of the oldest Cambrian melodies extant, and contains in the one volume the original publication to subscribers issued in two volumes at £2 2s. Notwithstanding the collections of Parry, Jones, Thomas and others, hundreds of old Cambrian melodies still remained scattered throughout the country in manuscripts, or were retained in the memory of harpists, Pennilion singers and others who loved and cherished the folk-songs of the past.

To collect some of these treasures, and rescue them from inevitable oblivion, says the compiler, has been to me a labour of love for more than half a century * * I secured many an old air of exquisite beauty from some venerable harpist, or aged Pennilion singer tottering on the brink of the grave

ENGLISH GLEE AND MADRIGAL WRITERS. By W. A. BARRETT. 8vo, cloth, 2s. 6d.

"Mr. Barrett is highly to be commended, no less for the vast amount of reliable information which he has collated upon the subject in hand, than for the concise manner in which, for the benefit of the reader, he has compressed it into a small space."—*Monthly Musical Record.*

NATIONAL SCHOOL OF OPERA IN ENGLAND. Being the Substance of a Paper read before the Licentiates of Trinity College, March, 1882. By FRANK AUSTIN. Post 8vo, sewed, 6d.

RATIONAL ACCOMPANIMENT TO THE PSALMS. By F. GILBERT WEBB. Post 8vo, 6d.

SONGS FROM THE RAVEL. (Words for Musical Setting.) A Book of Prose-Lyrics from Life and Nature. By ERNEST AUSTIN. Op. 30. Crown 8vo, sewed, 2s. 6d.

MODEST IDYLLS FOR MUSICAL SETTING. By ERNEST ALFIERI. 1s. net.

ÆSTHETICS, CRITICISMS, ESSAYS.

THE SYMPHONY WRITERS SINCE BEETHOVEN, Schubert, Schumann, Götz, Brahms, Tchaïkovsky, Brückner, Berlioz, Liszt, Strauss, Mahler, Mendelssohn, Saint-Saëns, etc. By FELIX WEINGARTNER. Translated by A. BLES. Many Portraits. Cr. 8vo, cloth, gilt top, 6s.

"Most stimulating and suggestive, full of acute thinking, of felicitous expression."—*New York.*

"The book is certainly well worth reading."—*Daily Chronicle.*

The author's intimate familiarity with the works he discusses lends a peculiar interest to the volume, which is certainly worthy a music lover's attention.

"A most fascinating book * * * the works of the various composers are critically discussed in regard to form and orchestration."—*Musical Star.*

GREATER WORKS OF CHOPIN. (Polonaises, Mazurkas, Nocturnes, etc.), and how they should be played. By J. KLECZYNSKI. Translated by Miss N. JANOTHA and Edited by SUTHERLAND EDWARDS. With Portrait, Facsimile, etc. Crown 8vo, cloth, 5s.

"A new book on Chopin which will doubtless receive a warm welcome from the lovers of the greatest genius of the pianoforte. * * * What gives this book a unique value of importance as a novelty is that it includes what is left of Chopin's notes for a pianoforte method which, brief as it is, contains some valuable and interesting hints which will benefit all pianists and students."—*New York Evening Post.*

MEZZOTINTS IN MODERN MUSIC. Brahms, Tchaïkovsky, Chopin, Strauss, Liszt and Wagner. By JAS. HUNEKER. Second Edition. Crown 8vo. cloth, gilt top, 7s. 6d.

CONTENTS.—The Music of the Future (Brahms)—A Modern Music Lord (Tschaikowsky)—Richard Strauss and Nietzsche—The Greater Chopin—A Liszt Etude—The Royal Road to Parnassus—A Note on Richard Wagner.

"Essays filled with literary charm and individuality, not self willed or over assertive but gracious and winning, sometimes profoundly contemplative, and anon frolicsome and more inclined to chaff than to instruct—but interesting and suggestive always."—*New York Tribune.*

THE PLACE OF SCIENCE IN MUSIC. By H. SAINT-GEORGE. Addressed to advanced students of that branch of musical knowledge commonly called Harmony. 8vo, sewed, 1s.

Mr. Baughan rejects the academic view of form as firmly as Mr. Saint-George rejects the academic view of harmony and counterpoint. The academics base their harmonic theories on laws of nature which Mr. Saint-George shows do not exist. . . . . Has joined Mr. Saint-George in the attack which will end in the total discomfiture of the academics.—J. F. RUNCIMAN in the *Saturday Review.*

MUSIC AND MUSICIANS. Essays and Criticisms, by ROBERT SCHUMANN. Translated, Edited and Annotated by F R. RITTER. Portrait of Robert Schumann, photographed from a Crayon by BENDEMANN. First Series 7th Edition. Thick cr. 8vo, cloth, 419 pages, 8s. 6d.

Ditto. Second Series, Third Edition. Thick crown 8vo cloth, 540 pages, 10s. 6d.

There are two sides to musical criticism, both equally interesting; the one, which is scientific analysis of musical form and treatment, possible only to experienced musicians, the other, which is the spiritual perception of the æsthetic side and influence of music, possible for any great mind whose perceptions are keenly cultivated in the highest canons of any art. Schumann represented the ideal musical critic, in that both of these essential points in criticism are to be found in his writings.—From the Introduction to "Ruskin on Music."

Scarcely find words sufficiently strong to express our delight * * * a book so rich in thought, so full of humour, so remarkable for its refined sarcasms, so original in its criticisms, so sprightly and elegant in language.—KARL MERZ in the *Musical World.*

The translations are vigorous and clear, and the exact sense of the originals, as far as possible, has been preserved.—*New York Musical Courier.*

A disquisition upon the value of Schumann's labour as an art critic seems quite uncalled for at the present date. Suffice it to say that it can hardly be over-estimated, and that his writings are as interesting and instructive at the present as they were when they were first penned.—*Monthly Musical Record.*

There is no use in trying to quote characteristic passages, because the volume is of such uniform merit and such continuous interest that it is impossible to make a selection. Musicians who take up the book will not find it easy to put it down again.—*Athenæum.*

Most fascinating reading, even to those who are not deeply versed in music.—*Westminster Review.*

Schumann was so just and fearless a critic, and his opinions are conspicuous for such sound judgment, that they are valuable in themselves altogether apart from the celebrity of their author. Some parts of the book will attract special notice, such, for instance, as the able defence of the then condemned Berlioz * * * * the book also contains notices of composers whom the world has forgotten.—*Music Trades' Review.*

MOZART'S DON GIOVANNI. A Commentary, from the Third French Edition of Charles Gounod. By W CLARK and J. T. HUTCHINSON. Crown 8vo, cloth, 3s. 6d

GOUNOD says in his Preface:—Don Giovanni, that unequalled and immortal masterpiece, that apogee of the lyrical drama, has attained a hundred years of existence and fame; it is popular, universally accepted and consecrated for ever. Is it understood? * * * Is it admired? Is it loved as it should be? The score of Don Giovanni has exercised the influence of a revelation upon the whole of my life; it has been and remains for me a kind of incarnation of dramatic and musical infallibility. I regard it as a work without blemish, of uninterrupted perfection, and this commentary is but the humble testimony of my veneration and gratitude to the genius to whom I owe the purest and most permanent joys of my life as a musician, etc.

THE DEEPER SOURCES OF THE BEAUTY AND EXPRESSION OF MUSIC. By JOSEPH GODDARD. Author of "Musical Development," "A Study of Gounod's Redemption," etc. With many Musical Examples. Crown 8vo, bevelled cloth, 3s. 6d.

CONTENTS.—CHAPTER I.—The Seeming Anomaly between the Human Origin of Music and its Elevated Beauty. CHAPTER II.—Abstract Musical, like Natural, Beauty is a Chance Fitness or Coincidence, of which the Visible Conditions are the Plasticity in Human Faculties and the Diversity in Outward Nature. CHAPTER III.—Timbre and Vowel-Sound briefly Analyzed; the Sensibility formed in the Ordinary Course of Natural Evolution to answer to them, lets into our Nature the World of Harmony. CHAPTER IV.—The Larger Reasons why Music is Free of the Objective World, and Discontinuous. CHAPTER V.—Contrast in Scenic Effect and in Music. CHAPTER VI.—The Source of those Distinct Suggestions of the General World which are Fundamental to the Musical Sensation—Position, Direction, Movement and Visual Form. CHAPTER VII.—The Second Factor in the Inherent Connection between Music and Motion: the Sense of the Horizontal latent in the Principle of Time. CHAPTER VIII.—Tonality. The Principles of Unity and Delimitation. CHAPTER IX.—Statement of the Full Case for the Explicability of Musical Expression from the Standpoint of the Influence of Speech. CHAPTER X.—Darwin's Hypothesis of Musical Expression. The Tendency of Music to Grow Old. The Influence of Inherited Feeling in the Effect upon us of Art and Nature. CHAPTER XI.—The Limitation involved in Music being the World of a Single Sense, is a Source of its Power. Statement of the Principle of Arbitrary Association. CHAPTER XII.—Summary and Concluding Remarks.

BEETHOVEN'S PIANOFORTE SONATAS Explained for the Lovers of the Musical Art. By ERNST VON ELTERLEIN. Translated by E. HILL, with Preface by ERNST PAUER. Entirely New and Revised Edition (the Sixth). With Portrait, Facsimile and View of Beethoven's House. Crown 8vo, cloth, 3s. 6d.

"He writes with the ripe knowledge and thorough understanding of a practical musician. Every musical student or amateur can safely trust him as a competent and agreeable guide. This English translation is most opportune, and will doubtless assist many a lover of Beethoven's music to appreciate more keenly the master's Sonatas."—E. PAUER.

BEETHOVEN'S SYMPHONIES in their Ideal Significance, Explained by ERNST VON ELTERLEIN. Translated by FRANCIS WEBER. With an Account of the Facts Relating to Beethoven's Tenth Symphony. By L. NOHL. Second Edition, with Portrait. Crown 8vo, cloth, 3s. 6d.

This small volume is intended in the first place, and more especially, for the earnest and thoughtful amateur, to whom it is to be a guide and companion in the artistic enjoyment and conscious appreciation of Beethoven's Symphonic Masterpieces. At the same time the work may not be unwelcome also to the practical musician.

HOW TO PLAY CHOPIN. The Works of Chopin and their proper Interpretation. By J. KLECZYNSKI. Translated by A. WHITTINGHAM. Fifth Edition. Woodcut and Music Illustrations. Post 8vo. cloth. 3s. 6d.

"Contains the cream of Chopin's instructions to his own pupils. To admirers of Chopin and players of his music we should say this book is indispensable "—*Bazaar.*

"It contains many interesting details and profitable hints. The author has much to tell us about the great pianist, as a teacher as well as a composer. Chopin as a composer remains to us as a heritage, but the tradition of his playing and teaching is naturally becoming every year more and more vague. So our author deserves praise for his attempt to snatch from oblivion any remembrances of the 'manner and touch' of the master."—*Academy.*

FROM LYRE TO MUSE. A History of the Aboriginal Union of Music and Poetry. By J. DONOVAN. Crown 8vo, cloth, 2s. 6d. net (pub. 5s.)

CHAPTERS:—1. Musical Impression. 2. History of Aboriginal Music. 3. Music and Individuality. 4. Fusion of Rhythm and Tones. 5. Fusion of Tones and Words. 6. How Harmony was Developed 7. Definition and Diagram of Evolution of Music.

SCHUMANN'S RULES AND MAXIMS. For young Musicians. Sewed, 2d.

"The 'Rules and Maxims' might have been entitled 'Proverbs,' for the truth of none of them can be called into question, and they give students the very best advice."—*Figaro.*

"A valuable store of hints and information, shrewdly written and pertinently put."—*Musical Opinion.*

BEETHOVEN'S SYMPHONIES Critically Discussed by A. TEETGEN. With Preface by JOHN BROADHOUSE. Second Edition. Post 8vo, cloth, 3s. 6d.

"We must say that many of his observations are not only acute but extremely just."—*Musical Times.*

"Mr. Teetgen gives evidence of deep knowledge of his hero's works, he supplies the reader with food for thought and reflection. We commend this little book to the attention of our readers."—*Musical Opinion.*

"Mr. Teetgen is a devout, though not a blind, worshipper of Beethoven." —*Musical Standard.*

PURITY IN MUSIC. By A. F. THIBAUT. Translated by J. BROADHOUSE. Crown 8vo, cloth, 2s. 6d.

CONTENTS.—1. On the Chorale. 2. Church Music other than the Choral. 3. Popular Melodies. 4. The Educating Influence of Good Models. 5. Effect. 6. On Judging the Works of Great Masters. 7. As to a Liberal Judgment. 8. On Perversions of Text. 9. Choral Societies.

SCHUMANN says:—"A fine book about music, read it frequently."

WOMAN AS A MUSICIAN. An Art Historical Study. By F. R. RITTER. 8vo, sewed, 1s.

BIOGRAPHICAL.

SOME MUSICAL RECOLLECTIONS OF FIFTY YEARS. By RICHARD HOFFMAN. With Memoir by MRS. HOFFMAN. Illustrated with many Plate Portraits. Crown 8vo, cloth, 6s. 1910

Delightful reminiscences of musicians and musical affairs in America and England. The account of Mendelssohn's leading of the "Elijah" at Manchester; of Jenny Lind and her appearance at Castle Garden and her tour of America under T. P. Barnum; of Thalberg, Von Bulow, Gottschalk, Liszt, and many others, and of the audiences and concerts throughout the country fifty years ago, makes most interesting reading.

VERDI: MAN AND MUSICIAN. His Biography, with especial Reference to his English Experience. Portraits by F. J. CROWEST. 8vo, cloth, 3s. 6d. net (pub. 7s. 6d.)

MOZART: THE STORY OF HIS LIFE AS MAN AND ARTIST. According to Authentic Documents and other Sources. By VICTOR WILDER. Translated by F. LIEBICH. To which is now added a Comprehensive Bibliography of Mozart Literature from every source, English and Foreign and a List of his Compositions Published and Unpublished. With 23 Portraits gathered from Various Sources. With Index. 2 volumes. Crown 8vo, cloth, 10s.

JAN. EV. ENGEL, *Imperial Librarian*, writing from the Mozarteum, Salz burg (Mozart's birthplace) on behalf of the Mozart Society, says:—

[*Translation.*]

I congratulate the publisher on the exemplary correctness of the edition and the author on having had at his disposal such rich and almost inexhaustible material from ancient down to most modern times, as foundation for his excellent work. This beautiful and valuable work, which has been translated with great thoroughness, has every right to a place *in the foremost ranks of English literature* to the honour of the great master whose life and work the gifted author has had presented to the English people in a most attractive way, besides conveying to them his appreciation of his (Mozart's) immortal compositions in a manner that has not been done previously in English.

"This biography in two handy volumes and published at a moderate price, will, we are sure, be warmly welcomed by the thousand and one admirers of one of the most astounding geniuses in musical history."—*Pall Mall Gazette.*

"Its merits are its enthusiasm, its judicious selection from an enormous mass of material, and its consecutiveness."—*Birmingham Gazette.*

ARTHUR SYMONS, in an appreciative notice in *The Saturday Review* said:—"The book is living, and to read it is to suffer over again this perfect and punished life."

BALFE: HIS LIFE AND WORKS. By W. A. BARRETT. Crown 8vo, bevelled cloth, 3s. 6d. net (pub. 7s. 6d.)

MUSICAL MEMORIES. By WILLIAM SPARK, *Mus.Doc. (late Organist of the Town Hall, Leeds).* Revised Popular Edition. With 16 Portraits. Thick crown 8vo, cloth. Published at 6s.

"A pleasantly written book of reminiscences of a large number of distinguished persons in the world of music . . . . Dr. Spark knows how to tell a good story, and has not a few new and old to tell: while the tone of his book is so invariably cheerful and good natured."—*Saturday Review.*

"The author speaks of things that he understands and of persons that he has known."—*St. James' Gazette.*

"Just one of those pleasant books which are instructive without being tedious, and amusing without being frivolous. The book is very pleasant reading and we counsel our readers to get it without delay."—*Musical Standard.*

TCHAIKOVSKY. His Life and Works. With Extracts from his Writings and the Diary of his Tour Abroad in 1888. By ROSA NEWMARCH. Edited with Additional Chapters by E. EVANS, 1908. With a Complete Classific Account of Works, Copious Analyses of Important Works, Analytical and other Indices; also Supplement dealing with "The Relation of Tchaïkovsky to Art-Questions of the Day." Portrait and Index. Thick crown 8vo, cloth, gilt top, 7s. 6d.

"The chapters written by Mr. Edwin Evans, Senr., are excellent and should be perused with attention, as they denote a keen, critical insight and a broad outlook on matters generally. * * * The popularity of Tchaïkovsky in England is certainly not on the wane, and the present volume will doubtless be welcomed by the many admirers of the Russian master."—*Morning Post.*

"A well planned and in parts fascinating study of a composer whose rare charm of melodic beauty and fine sense of musical proportion have completely captured the taste of the time * * * It is the fullest and most authoritative monograph of Tchaikovsky available for English readers."—*The Scotsman.*

"Issued from the Press which in recent years has given to the musical world so much that is of intrinsic value—that of the firm of William Reeves, publisher of *The Musical Standard*—this volume, dedicated 'to Henry J. Wood, who has helped to realise so many of Tchaikovsky's masterpieces, and to his wife,' is first in the field in thoroughness and in style. * * * is so presented as to be of absorbing interest to the ordinary lover of music, of value to the student, and indispensable to such as desire to have at hand reliable analyses of the compositions of the greatest of Russian composers. Rosa Newmarch is perhaps responsible to a greater degree than anyone in this country for bringing under notice Tchaikovsky. To her pen is due the best and ripest of the original matter the volume contains; although the work of Mr. Edwin Evans is also of such a character as to merit high praise. * * * Tchaïkovsky was a world artist and he speaks in a language that is growingly appreciated by the scholars of all nations. * * The volume will assuredly rank among the standard works relating to musical art."—*Sheffield Daily Independent.*

NOTICE OF ANTHONY STRADIVARI. The celebrated Violin Maker known by the name of Stradivarius, preceded by Historical and Critical Researches on the origin and Transformations of Bow Instruments, and followed by a Theoretical Analysis of the Bow and Remarks on Francis Tourte. By F. J. FETIS. Translated by J. BISHOP. Facsimile of a Letter of Stradivarius. 8vo, cloth, 5s.

The greater part of the matter in above is the work of M. Vuillaume, who spent the greater part of his life in studying the principles which guided Stradivarius in his labours. With the aid of Fétis and his additional suggestions and matter the now celebrated work was produced.

CHOPIN: THE MAN AND HIS MUSIC. By JAMES HUNEKER. Author of "Mezzotints in Modern Music." With Musical Examples. Thick crown 8vo, cloth, 10s.

"Mr. Huneker is a Chopin enthusiast. He accords admiration to Brahms, to Wagner, to Tchaïkovsky: his worship is reserved for Chopin. Being gifted with clear insight and imagination which grasp many and diverse moods Mr. Huneker is a sane critic and a manly. . . . . There is no pretence at new material in the book. Mr. Huneker has garnered all that has been written about the composer and he has threshed out the grain from the chaff. The result is, therefore, of value."—*Musical Standard.*

"The volume will at once take its place in the front rank of books on Chopin. . . . . . the masterly chapter of 74 pages on the etudes will soon be found indispensable by all teachers and students of the pianoforte."—*The Nation (U.S.A.)*

"A work of unique merit, of distinguished style, of profound insight and sympathy and of the most brilliant literary quality."—*The New York Times.*

"Of works on Chopin published since Niecks' life, this is by far the most important."—G. C ASHTON JONSON in "A Handbook to Chopin's Works."

LIFE OF CHOPIN. By FRANZ LISZT. New and very much Enlarged Edition. Translated in full now for the first time by JOHN BROADHOUSE. Crown 8vo, cloth, 6s.

GEORGE SAND describes it as "un peu exuberent en style, mais rempli de bonnes choses et de très belles pages."

G. C. ASHTON JONSON says in his "Handbook to Chopin's Works":—"For the personal reminiscences of one of the greatest composers by one of the greatest executive artists of the world must be invaluable to the Chopin student."

"Franz Liszt has written a charming sketch of Chopin's life and art."—*Ency. Brit.*

"Liszt's criticisms upon his separate works have all the eloquent mysticisms to be expected from him; and the biography is a book musicians will always prize."—*Sunday Times.*

"It will afford the student the greatest help in understanding the undercurrent of emotion which characterises the works of Chopin."—*Morning Post*

"Let us therefore contribute one good word to help it forward, as we would tend a flower which springs up spontaneously over the grave of one we love."—*Musical Times.*

FREDERIC CHOPIN: HIS LIFE AND LETTERS. B Moritz Karasowski. Translated by E. Hill. Ne Edition Revised and further Letters added writte during the composer's Sojourn in England and Scot land, 1848-9. Second and Revised Edition. With Portraits and a Facsimile. 2 volumes. Crown 8vo bevelled cloth, 10s.

"Chopin is and remains the boldest and proudest poetic spirit of th age."—Robert Schumann.

"A book with which all students of Chopin must needs be acquainte It contains a good deal of first hand information and is our only sour for many valuable documents."—*The Guardian.*

The author in his Preface says:—Several years of friendship with t family of Frederic Chopin have enabled me to have access to his letters ar to place them before the public. . . . In compliance with the wishes many of Chopin's friends and admirers I have undertaken to sketch h career from the materials afforded me by his one surviving sister, from h letters, etc. . . . in this work which contains full particulars about Chopin youth I have corrected the erroneous dates and mis-statements which ha found their way into all the German and French periodicals and books.

Grove's *Dictionary of Musicians* says:—The truth about Chopin's birt family, health, character, friendships, early training, and the dawn of h career as a player and composer was not known until the publication Moritz Karasowski's recent and trustworthy biography.

"The first serious attempt at a Biography of Chopin."—Prof. Niecks.

"Gives bits of information found nowhere else and the Letters of Chop make the book invaluable to those who would really know the Poli master."—*Musical America.*

MAKERS OF MUSIC. Biographical Sketches of the Gre Composers. With Chronological Summaries of the Works and Facsimiles from Musical MSS. of Bac Handel, Purcell, Dr. Arne, Gluck, Haydn, Mozart, Bee hoven, Weber, Schubert, Berlioz, Mendelssohn, Chopi Schumann, Wagner, Verdi, Gounod, Brahms and Grei with General Chronological Table. By R. Farquharso Sharp. Portrait of Purcell. Third Edition. Crow 8vo, cloth, 5s.

The author's endeavour throughout this work has been to convey an i pression of the personality of each composer, as well as to furnish bi graphical detail. At the end of each biography is a tabulated list of t composer's works and dates of production, together with a facsimile fro one of his original manuscripts. A useful volume, got up in good style ar well adapted for a gift or prize. Has speedily run into three editions.

TEMPLETON AND MALIBRAN. Reminiscences of the Renowned Singers, with Original Letters and An dotes. Three Authentic Portraits by Mayall. 8v cloth, 2s. 6d.

CHOPIN: AS REVEALED BY EXTRACTS FROM HIS DIARY. By COUNT TARNOWSKI. Translated from the Polish by N. JANOTHA. With Eight Portraits. Crown 8vo, bevelled cloth, 2s. 6d. net (or paper cover 1s. 6d. net).

"Throws many curious sidelights on the character of the great composer."—*Sunday Sun.*

"The notes on Chopin were written by special request and under the direction of Princess Marceline Czartoryska. From her, Count Tarnowski received many interesting details as well as letters written by Chopin, in which the master alludes to many of his compositions as well as to the conditions under which they were written. Really an absorbing little tome, etc."—*Musical Standard.*

BEETHOVEN. By RICHARD WAGNER. With a Supplement from the Philosophical Works of Arthur Schopenhauer. Trans. by EDWARD DANNREUTHER. Third Edition. Crown 8vo, cloth, 6s.

"This characteristic essay, a written exposition of Wagner's thoughts on the significance of the master's music, may be read with advantage by all students."—W. H. WEBBE in *The Pianist's A. B. C.*

"It is a plain duty to be familiar and even intimate with the opinion of one famous man about another. Gladly therefore we welcome Mr. Dannreuther's translation of the work before us. Mr. Dannreuther has achieved his task with the conscientiousness of his nature and with a success due to much tact and patience."—*Musical Times.*

BIOGRAPHICAL DICTIONARY OF FIDDLERS. Including Performers on the Violoncello and Double Bass, Past and Present. Containing a Sketch of their Artistic Career, together with Notes of their Compositions. By A. MASON CLARKE. 9 Portraits. Post 8vo, bevelled cloth, 5s.

"We may here take the opportunity of recommending a useful book to all lovers of violins and violinists. Fiddlers, Ancient and Modern, is practically a little Biographical Dictionary, well arranged with some excellent portraits."—*Northern Whig.*

CHERUBINI. Memorials illustrative of his Life. By E. BELLASIS. Thick crown 8vo, cloth, 6s.

The standard biography of Cherubini.

FRANZ LISZT. By T. CARLAW MARTIN. 12mo, bound, 1s. (paper, 6d.)

LIFE OF BEETHOVEN. By LOUIS NOHL. Translated by JOHN J. LALOR. Third Edition. With Portraits and Facsimile. Crown 8vo, bevelled cloth, gilt edges, 3s. 6d.

"A standard biography."

SKETCHES OF ENGLISH GLEE COMPOSERS. Historical Biographical and Critical. From about 1735-1866. By D. BAPTIE. Post 8vo, bevelled cloth, 5s.

LIFE AND WORKS OF MOZART. By A. WHITTINGHAM Cloth, 1s. 6d. (or paper, 1s.)

LIFE AND WORKS OF HANDEL. By A. WHITTINGHAM Cloth, 1s. 6d. (or paper, 1s.)

THE BACH LETTERS. Letters of Samuel Wesley, relatin to the Introduction into England of the Works of Bach Ed. by E. WESLEY. Second Edition. 8vo, cloth, 2s. 6d

DICTIONARY OF 4,000 BRITISH MUSICIANS. From th Earliest Times. By F. J. CROWEST. Crown 8vo, clotl 2s. (paper, 1s.)

A Dictionary of British Musicians—a work devoted exclusively to tl names of native composers, instrumentalists, vocalists, writers, etc., wl have contributed to the making of English musical art from the earlie times to the present. Blank spaces are left to each letter for any add tional names to be written in.

PURCELL. By WILLIAM H. CUMMINGS, *Mus.Doc.* Crowı 8vo, cloth, 2s. 6d.

The only available life of this great English musician. Dr. Cumming spared no time or trouble in making it as far as possible a complete an exhaustive treatise.

CHERUBINI. By F. J. CROWEST. Crown 8vo, cloth, 2s. 6d

CONTENTS:—Birth and Parentage—Under Sarti—Earliest Works—Visit London—*Lodoiska*—*Medée*—*Les Deux Journées*—*Faniska*—Berlioz and *A. Baba*—Cherubini's Overtures—A Sacred Music Composer—Mass in F—Mass in D minor—Mass in C—Requiem in C minor—Requiem in D mino—Cherubini's Prolificness—At Catel's Grave—Death, Obsequies and Caree—His Influence upon Music—Estimate of his Dramatic Works—Of hi Sacred Works—Influence as a Teacher—Temperament and Disposition-Anecdotes of Cherubini—Catalogue of Compositions—Index.

SKETCHES OF GREAT VIOLINISTS AND GREAT PIAN ISTS. Biographical and Anecdotal, with Account (the Violin and Early Violinists. Viotti, Spohr, Paga nini, De Beriot, Ole Bull, Clementi, Moscheles, Schı mann (Robert and Clara), Chopin, Thalberg, Gottschall Liszt. By G. T. FERRIS. Second Edition. Crown 8v(bevelled cloth, 3s. 6d. (or cloth, gilt edges, 4s. 6d.)

A very useful book for a prize or gift.

PORTRAIT GALLERIES.

SIXTY YEARS OF MUSIC. A Record of the Art in England during the Victorian Era. Containing 70 Portraits of the most Eminent Musicians. Oblong quarto, boards, cloth back, 2s. 6d.

NATIONAL PORTRAIT GALLERY OF BRITISH MUSICIANS. By JOHN WARRINER, Mus.D. Trinity College, Dublin. Introduction by JOSEPH BENNETT. Over 500 Photo Portraits of well-known and eminent living Musicians of Great Britain and Ireland, with short Biographical notice of each. The whole bound in one handsome oblong folio volume, cloth lettered. Offered for 7s. 6d. net (published 14s. net).

REEVES' CATALOGUE OF MUSIC AND MUSICAL LITERATURE. Ancient and Modern, Second-Hand and New; containing the Contents of Libraries recently purchased, with a large quantity of Curious, Scarce, and Useful Music: Full Scores, Organ Music, Duets, Trios, Quartetts, Quintetts, Sextetts, Septetts, etc.; Tutors, Historical, Theoretical and Biographical Works in English, French, German, Italian, Spanish, Dutch, etc., including some Works of the greatest rarity and value. On Sale for Cash. This Catalogue sent post free on application.

"Mr. W. Reeves, who has established his claim to be regarded as the recognized publisher of English Musical Literature, has a strong list of books for the amateur and the professor."—*Publishers' Circular.*

"The best and safest method for the inexperienced to adopt, is to make application to some leading and trustworthy publisher of musical books of the class in question, relying on his judgment and the traditions of his house to supply what is genuine and suitable. Without being invidious, we may say that such a publisher is Mr. W. Reeves."—*Bazaar.*

HISTORY.

THE MUSIC OF THE MOST ANCIENT NATIONS. Particularly of the Assyrians, Egyptians and Hebrews; with special reference to recent discoveries in Western Asia and in Egypt. By Carl Engel. With numerous Illustrations and Index. Thick 8vo, cloth. Published at 18s., now offered for 8s. 6d. net.

Contents:—Chapter I.—The Oldest Records on Music. Representations of Musical Instruments on Ancient Sculptures and Paintings—National Music applied to Ethnology—Monumental Records referring to Assyrian Music—The Ruins of Nimroud, Khorsabad and Kouyunjik—The Extent to which the characteristics of Assyrian Music can be Ascertained from the Representations of the Instruments—The Gradual Development of Music from its Most Primitive State, demonstrated by a Comparison of the Music of Modern Nations in Different Stages of Civilization—The Earliest Musical Instruments—Examples of Musical Scales in Use among Nations in Different Stages of Civilization—The Earliest Development of Vocal Music—The Degree of Progress in Music attained by the Assyrians —Their Accomplishments in other Arts. Chapter II.—Musical Instruments of the Assyrians. The Harp—Traces of the Ancient Oriental Harp in Europe—The Assyrian Lyre and the Nubian Kissar—The Assyrian Dulcimer and the Persian Santir—The Asor—The Tamboura or Guitar—The Double-pipe—The Trumpet—The Drum—Assyrian Bronze Bells found in the Ruins of Nimroud—Tambourine and Cymbals—Remarks on the Dancing of the Assyrian Musicians—Traces of some other Assyrian Instruments—Conjectures on the Antiquity of Stringed Instruments Played with a Bow—Some Peculiar Similarities between Ancient Asiatic and European Instruments—The Names of Musical Instruments. Chapter III. —Assyrian Musical Performances. Various Combinations of Musical Instruments—Description of the Assyrian Bas-reliefs in the British Museum on which Musical Performers are Represented—Other Representations of Assyrian Musicians briefly Described—The Characteristics of the Performances—Fondness of the Assyrians for Music—Their Songs—Music employed in their Religious Worship—Court Bands of the Kings—Rhythmical Character of the Music—Oriental Music of the Present Time—Choruses of the Dervishes—Call to Prayer of the Muezzin—Character of the Assyrian Instrumental Accompaniments—Harmony not Entirely Unknown to the Assyrians. Chapter IV.—Musical System of the Assyrians. Resemblance of the Assyrian Music to that of other Ancient Oriental Nations—The Pentatonic Scale—The Present Existence of the Pentatonic Scale in various Asiatic Nations evidenced by Tunes from China, Siam, Java, Hindoostan, Burmah and Japan—High Antiquity of the Pentatonic Scale in Asia—The Order of Intervals in which the Assyrian Stringed Instruments appear to have been usually Tuned—Traces of the Pentatonic Scale among the Ancient Greeks—The Intervals of the Nubian Kissar—Subdivisions of the Whole Tone—Diffusion of the Pentatonic Scale—The Pentatonic Scale of the Ancient American Indians—Traces of the same Scale in the Music of the Scotch and other Celtic Races —The Peculiar Character of the Assyrian Music—The Probable Musical Notation of the Assyrians. Chapter V.—Music of the Ancient Egyptians

Egyptian Instruments—Various Harps—Bruce's Harps—Egyptian name of the Harp—The Trigonon—The Lyre—The Tamboura—Peculiar Stringed Instruments—Pipes, Flutes, Double-pipes—Trumpets—Drums and Tambourines—Curious Instruments of Percussion—The Sistrum—Crotala, Cymbals, Bells—Vocal and Instrumental Performances—The Egyptian Musical Instruments compared with the Assyrian—Opinions of some Musical Historians. CHAPTER VI.—MUSIC OF THE HEBREWS. Gradual Development of the Hebrew Music—Musical Instruments—Diversity of Opinion respecting the Real Nature of some of the Hebrew Instruments—Josephus' Account—The Chatzozerah—The Shophar—The Magrepha—Nebel and Nofre—The Hebrew Lyre—Vocal and Instrumental Performances—Hebrew Music of the Present Day—Literature of Hebrew Music—Eastern Origin of our own Music.

Grove's Dictionary says of Carl Engel:

"His attainments as a musician, his clear insight into books in many languages, his indefatigable perseverance in research, and the exercise of a rare power of judicious discrimination, made him one of the first authorities on his subject in Europe, he became a collector when opportunities were more frequent than they are now for acquiring rare instruments and books. He thus formed a private museum and library that could hardly be rivalled except by a few public institutions."

CHRONOMETRICAL CHART OF MUSICAL HISTORY. Presenting a Bird's Eye View from the Pre-Christian Era to the XXth Century. By C. A. HARRIS, A.R.C.O., etc. On linen, folded in case, 2s. net (on special paper, 1s. net).

PROF. PROUT says:—I have examined your chart with great interest, both plan and execution seem to me to be excellent. You have managed to get a wonderful amount of information into a very small space. I think the Chart should be most useful and cordially wish you success.

DR. T. H. YORKE TROTTER, *Principal, London Academy of Music:* "Extremely well got up and will be useful."

DR. F. J. KARN, *Principal, London College of Music:* "Your very useful chart . . . . extremely well drawn up, showing in a compact form a great deal of information, and is a useful comparative form. Several professors have expressed delight with it."

Trinity College, London: "The Library Committee desire me to express their most cordial thanks for the donation of a copy of a 'Chronometrical Chart of Musical History' to the College library."—SHELLEY FISHER, *Secretary.*

"Like a Bovril tabloid—much nourishment in a little room."—HEAD MISTRESS, *South African School.*

"Sure to be very useful to students . . . excellently arranged and seems to be very accurate and thorough."—DR. RALPH DUNSTAN.

"Excellent chart . . . and is certainly valuable in helping the imagination to grasp synchronous events."—H. OSMOND ANDERTON, ESQ., *Librarian to Birmingham and Midland Institute School of Music.*

HISTORY OF HUNGARIAN MUSIC. By J. KALDY (*Director of the Royal Hungarian Opera).* Crown 8vo, bevelled cloth, 2s. 6d. net.

"Information not to be had anywhere else . . . . . should be on every musical shelf."—*Internationale Musikgesellschaft.*

THE GROWTH AND DEVELOPMENT OF MUSIC. Described in Chapters on the Study of Musical History. By EDWARD DICKINSON. With an Annotated Guide to Music Literature. Over 400 pp. Thick 8vo, cloth, 10s.

CHAPTERS:—1. Primitive Music. 2. Music of the Ancient Cultured Nations: Assyrians, Egyptians, Hebrews, Greeks and Romans. 3. Song in the Early Christian Church. 4. The Catholic Liturgy. 5. The Catholic Liturgic Chant. 6. Beginnings of Polyphonic Music. Popular Music in the Middle Ages. 7. The Age of the Netherlanders, 1400-1550. 8. Choral Music of the Sixteenth Century. 9. Early German Protestant Music. 10. Protestant Church Music in England. 11. The Madrigal—The Opera—Modern Tonality. 12. Early Growth of Instrumental Music. 13. The Violin and its Music: First Stages of the Suite and Sonata. 14. Keyed Chamber Instruments: Progress of the Clavier Suite and Sonata. 15. The Italian Opera in the Seventeenth Century. 16 The Opera Buffa, Seventeenth and Eighteenth Centuries. 17. Rise of the Opera in France, Seventeenth Century. 18. Italian Opera Seria in the Eighteenth Century. 19. Introduction of the Italian Dramatic Forms into German Religious Music. 20. Johann Sebastian Bach, 1685-1750. 21. Handel, 1685-1759. 22. Opera-Comique in the Eighteenth Century. 23. Gluck, 1714-1787. 24. Haydn, 1732-1809. 25. Mozart, 1756-1791. 26. Beethoven, 1770 1827. 27. The German Romantic Opera. Weber, 1786-1826. 28. The German Lied. Schubert, 1797-1828. 29. Piano Playing to about 1830. 30. Schumann, 1810-1856. 31. Mendelssohn, 1809-1847. 32. Chopin, 1809-1849. 33. Programme Music. 34. Berlioz, 1803-1869. 35. Liszt, 1811-1886. 36. The Opera in the Nineteenth Century to about 1850. I. Italian Opera. 37. The Opera in the Nineteenth Century to about 1850. II. French Opera. 38. Wagner, 1813-1883. 39. Recent Music in Germany and Austria. 40. Recent Music in France. 41. Recent Music in Italy. 42. Recent Music in Russia, Bohemia and Scandinavia. 43. Recent Music in England and America. Bibliographical List. Index.

MR. DICKINSON in his Preface says:—The vastness and complexity of the study of the history of music are bewildering to those who enter upon it unassisted. This volume is intended to clear the way by indicating the problems, the method and the materials. The narrative and critical portion gives a terse and comprehensive summary of music history, showing what are the important subjects involved and their connections and relations. The bibliographical sections lead the student to the best critical commentaries in the English language on every phase and detail of the subject.

"Mr. Dickinson has written a book of unquestionable value . . . . . the author's critical judgment is highly discriminating."—*Musical Standard.*

MR. ERNEST NEWMAN in the *Manchester Guardian* writes:—Mr. Dickinson has had the excellent idea of furnishing the musical student with a guide to the best literature in English upon the Art . . . . . For Mr. Dickinson's general treatment of his subject one can have nothing but praise. His method is to take each stage in the development of music separately, characterise it in a short but highly concentrated chapter and then give references to the complete English literature upon the subject. His summaries are models of sound judgment and swift statement, not more than once or twice, perhaps, could one find fault with either their completeness in every essential point or their cool and Catholic impartiality. The bibliographical guides are practically as full as they could be made. . . . . the total omissions are exceedingly trifling, while the extent and the accuracy of the information conveyed make the book indispensable to *students* and to *public libraries.*

MANUAL OF MUSICAL HISTORY. From the Epoch of Ancient Greece to our present time. By Dr. F. L. Ritter. Second Edition. Cr. 8vo, bevelled cloth, 2s. 6d.

"An agreeably and cogently written volume, dealing with a variety of topics which bear more or less directly on the history of music."—W. H. Webbe in *The Pianist's A. B. C*

"Portable and well arranged * * * well up to-date and contains a useful index. Students preparing for examinations will find the book distinctly serviceable."—*Teacher's Times*.

CATECHISM OF MUSICAL HISTORY AND BIOGRAPHY. By F. J. Crowest. Revised and Enlarged Edition. Tenth Thousand. 187 pp. Post 8vo, cloth, 2s. (paper, 1s.)

This work gives special attention to English musicians, and is brought down to 1905.

Musical Education says:—"An excellent little book—yet not so little since it contains an immense amount of information—historical, biographical and critical—in a very small compass."

THE STUDENT'S HISTORY OF MUSIC. History of Music, from the Christian Era to the present time. By Dr. F. L. Ritter. Third Edition. 478 pages of Letterpress and 72 Plates of Musical Illustrations. Thick crown 8vo, cloth, 7s. 6d.

"To such as are preparing for examination this valuable work must render great service."—*Christian Age*.

"A reliable guide to those students who as he says 'feel the desire, the want, of a deeper and more general knowledge of and information as to, the growth and progress of their art than is common.' That this intention has been successfully carried out in the present volume we can conscientiously affirm."—*Musical Times*.

"With the exception of Mr. Hullah's Lectures, we can recall no book in the English language of recent date which attempts to cover the same ground. Both as useful to the student as a work of reference, and as interesting and instructive to the general reader on musical subjects, this work of Professor Ritter may confidently be recommended."—*Monthly Musical Record*.

A HISTORY OF PIANOFORTE MUSIC. With Critical Estimates of its Greatest Masters and Sketches of their Lives. By John C. Fillmore. Edited with an Introductory Preface by Ridley Prentice. Crown 8vo, cloth, 3s. 6d.

Synopsis:—The Pianoforte and its Immediate Precursors (the Harpsichord and Clavichord)—Polyphonic Music (Bach, Handel, D. Scarlatti)—Homophonic Music (E. Bach, Haydn, Mozart)—The Emotional Content of Music (Beethoven)—The Classic and the Romantic in Music (Weber, Schubert, Mendelssohn, Chopin and Schumann)—Technique of the First Classical Period—Technique of the Second Classical Period—Technique of the Transition Period—Technique of the Romantic Period—Minor Composers and Virtuosi of the Different Epochs—Index.

Dudley Buck says of it:—"In my judgment the work should be in the hands of every earnest student."

"The only work of its kind in English. It groups the composers and their works into epochs and gives a clear description of the different epochs. It contains an interesting account of the lives of all the greatest composers and their works."—*Etude*.

THE RISE OF MUSIC. Being a Careful Enquiry into the Development of the Art from its Primitive Puttings forth in Egypt and Assyria to its Triumphant Consummation in Modern Effect. Especially bringing out the Influence of the Church upon the Joint Development of Harmony and Notation—the Importance of that Great Central Development the Enweavement of the Scales—the Creative Consequences of the Clavier Type of Instrument and the Explanation of a New and Perfect Order of Beauty resting upon our Tempered System. By JOSEPH GODDARD. With Illustrations of early Instruments and numerous Musical Examples drawn from Ancient and Modern Sources. With Index. Thick crown 8vo, cloth, gilt top, 7s. 6d.

It will be seen that this work is not a history of music in the ordinary sense, but rather a tracing of the organic unfolding of the musical art. At the same time it presents a perspective of both the history and constitution of music, in which history is seen to elucidate theory and theory history.

Readers will greatly appreciate the numerous musical examples culled from all sources which appear throughout the book.

"Musical enthusiasts, whom the technical language of their art does not appal, will delight in this scholarly book. Mr. Goddard's object is to show that music, commonly regarded as the youngest of the arts, had its roots in primeval man, but needed a longer time to develop into a fully constituted art than did painting and literature. It was comparatively easy for the painter to perfect his art. He had his model, Nature, always before him. The poet, in like manner, once he possessed an alphabet, had only to look around him to find the grandest subjects ready to his pen. But the musician had to discover and fix his own rules and principles, slowly revealed to him by the march of science and by chance inventions. The ancient Egyptians, for instance, used the flute, lyre and harp, but, as Mr. Goddard points out, the mass of our modern musical forms date only from the invention of the clavier type of instrument, a little over a couple of centuries ago. Modern dramatic music, too, springs as an art form largely from the light interludes played in the Italian theatres only two centuries ago. Mr. Goddard's book is well illustrated and should find a place in many a musical home."—*The Christian World.*

AN ACCOUNT OF THE RISE OF MILITARY MUSIC IN ENGLAND and Memoirs of the Royal Artillery Band, its Origin, History and Progress. By H. G. FARMER. With 14 Illustrations. 8vo, cloth, 5s.

The Records of the R.A. Band date as far back as 1762, and its history may fairly be stated to represent the growth of the military band.

The First Music Printed from Engraved Plates in England.

PARTHENIA Or the First Musick ever Printed for the Virginals. Composed by three famous Masters, William Byrd, Dr. John Bull and Orlando Gibbons. Translated into Modern Notation and Edited by E. F. Rimbault, LL.D., F.S.A. With Fac-similes of the original Engraved Title, showing a Lady playing the Virginals, a page of the Music, and the Curious and Interesting Dedication. Followed by the whole of the Music arranged for Playing on the Piano in the Modern Notation this forming a further 50 pages. Together with an account of the Virginals, Method of Playing, Early References, etc. By Dr. Rimbault. This Reprint limited to 250 copies only. Folio, gilt top, rough edges, imitation old boards, cloth back lettered To Subscribers, 12s. 6d. (pub. 21s.)

The Virginal or Virginals from Henry the Seventh's time to nearly the close of the 17th century, included all quilled Keyboard instruments, the Harpsichord, Spinet, etc. Henry the Eight, according to a contemporary, played well on the Virginals. Queen Mary is said to have equalled if not surpassed Queen Elizabeth in music playing, the Regals and Lute as well as the Virginals. The first music for this tribe of instruments—including the Harpsichord—was the "Parthenia." It consists principally of "Pavans and "Galliards," in common use for dancing purposes in Queen Elizabeth's time, "Preludiums," "Fantazia of Foure Parts," etc.

The printing of music from engraved copper plates is supposed to have begun at Rome where a collection of Canzonets was engraved by Simone Verovio in 1586. In France towards the end of Louis XIV.'s reign the great house of Ballard began to make use of engraving, some of Lully's operas being printed from type and some from engraved copper plates. The Germans, of course, practised the art, one early book of Exercises being composed and engraved by the great John Sebastian Bach himself. In England "Parthenia" was the first produced, appearing in 1611.

Virdung in 1511 is the oldest authority mentioning the virginals, but Rimbault quotes the following proverb that was formerly inscribed on a wall of the Manor House of Leckingfield, Yorkshire, and if, as thought to be, as old as the time of Henry the Seventh (1485-1509) contains a reference earlier than Virdung:

"A Slac Strynge in a Virginall soundithe not aright,
It doth abide no wrestinge it is so loose and light;
The sound board crasede, forsith the instrumente,
Throw misgovernance to make notes which was not his intente."

THE PAST AND THE FUTURE. Inaugural Lecture at Gresham College, Nov., 1890. By J. Frederick Bridge. Mus. Doc. Crown 8vo. sewed. 6d.

THE WORLD'S EARLIEST MUSIC. Traced to its Beginnings in Ancient lands. By collected Evidences o Relics, Records, History and Musical Instruments, fror Greece, Etruria, Egypt, China, through Assyria an Babylonia to the Primitive Home, the Land of Akka and Sumer. By HERMANN SMITH. With 65 full pag Illustrations and Cuts, nearly 400 pp. Crown 8vc cloth, 6s.

"I return the sheets you entrusted to me of 'The World's Earlie Music.' There is nothing I could criticize in those interesting pages."-A. J. HIPKINS in a letter to the Author.

"Should be in the hands of every musician. . . . . Most interesting i his Chapter upon the music of Japan."—*Pall Mall Gazette.*

"Technically though it occasionally must be, the book is one whic should charm all music lovers."—*Morning Leader.*

"The book, which is profusely illustrated, is most interesting, and is, i its handsome cloth binding, well worth its published price, 6/-"—*Th Musical Star.*

"I confess to a very considerable ignorance, natural and acquired, c the ancient instruments; but it seems to me that Mr. Smith has got as nea the truth as a twentieth-century mortal can."—J. F. RUNCIMAN in *Th Saturday Review.*

"It is a pleasantly written volume dealing with the earliest condition of music in ancient lands. From rock carvings, wall paintings, tablet and vases, sculptures, papyri and so forth, Mr. Smith has drawn th materials for a volume which has involved an immense amount of researc and contains a vast quantity of information conveyed in a very lucid an readable manner."—H. A. SCOTT in *The Academy.*

"No more enthusiastic worker, nor patient student, exists than Mi Hermann Smith. The structure, character and capabilities of every kin of musical instrument have been the objects of his study for many year To an intense love of his subjects he adds *an attractive style.* . . . Th liking of the ear in music is a liking by inheritance, transmitted as facial type is. This view is new, etc."—*Birmingham Daily Post.*

ON CONDUCTING. By Richard Wagner. Translated b E. Dannreuther. Second Edition, cr. 8vo, cloth, 5s

A Treatise on Style in the Execution of Classical Music, written by practical master of the grand style.

Weingartner, speaking of this celebrated work, says:—"Wagner's boo laid the foundation for a new understanding of the function of the co ductor, in whom we now recognise, not only the eternal factor that hol together an orchestral, choral or operatic performance, but above all tl spiritualising internal factor that gives the performance its very soul."

Grove's Dictionary says: "One of the finest of his minor publication and to a professional musician perhaps the most instructive. A Treati on *Style*, giving his views as to the true way of rendering classical musi with minute directions how to do it and how not to do it, together wi many examples in musical type from the instrumental works of Beethove Weber, Mozart, etc."

NOTES ON CONDUCTING AND CONDUCTORS. By T. R Croger, F.R.G.S., F.Z.S., also the Organising and Con ducting of Amateur Orchestras, with three full-pag Illustrations of the Various "Beats" and Plan of th Orchestra. Third Edition, Revised and Enlarged Crown 8vo, cloth, 2s. (paper, 1s.)

"A mine of good things."—*Musical Opinion.*

"One of the best guides to conducting."—*Music Trades Review.*

"A capital little book brightly written and full not only of entertainin and racily-told anecdotes, but also of clear and sensibly-expressed opinion on musical matters."—*The Stage.*

"The book appeals particularly to conductors of provincial societie whether instrumental or choral; it is written in a pleasant style, and i full of practical hints by one who knows his subject well."—*Monthl Musical Record.*

"Many practical hints on the organizing and conducting of amateu orchestras and choral societies."—*Morning Post.*

HOW TO PLAY FROM SCORE. Treatise on Accompani ment from Score on the Organ or Pianoforte. By F Fetis. Translated by A. Whittingham. With 40 page of Musical Examples. Crown 8vo, bevelled cloth, 3s. 6d

Contents:—Introduction. 1. On the Different Arrangements of Voice and Instruments in Scores (Partitions). 2. On Vocal Parts; Instrument Parts, their Fixed Pitch and the Manner in which they are Written. 3 Concerning the Manner in which the Accompanist should Read a Score i order to grasp its Substance and its Details. 4. The Mechanism of Ac companiment. 5. Concerning the Influence of the Accompanist on th Vocalist. 6. On Difference of Style. 7. On the Accompaniment of Earl Music without Orchestra, the Duets and Trios of Clari, Durante, Hand and the Psalms of Marcello. 8. On the Reproduction of Ancient Orche tral Accompaniments. 9. On the Modern Style of Accompaniment. 10. O Mozart, Cherubini, Mehul, Spontini, Rossini and the Modern School. 1 Conclusion.

This popular and useful book might have been entitled "The Art o Making Arrangements for the Organ or Pianoforte from Full Orchestr and other Scores." It contains all that is necessary to know upon th subject.

ORGAN.

THE ORGAN FIFTY YEARS HENCE. A Study of its Development in the Light of its Past History and Present Tendencies. By FRANCIS BURGESS, *F.S.A., Scot.* 8vo, 1s. net.

"All organists should read Mr. Francis Burgess' lecture on 'The Organ Fifty Years Hence.' We have every sympathy for the opinions Mr. Burgess expresses, though we have our doubts as to whether the unpopularity of electric action is not fully justified, etc."—*The Church Union Gazette.*

"Gives us an excellent summary of what has been and is being done towards improvement in organ construction and tone, and his criticisms are always sound and convincing."—*Glasgow Herald.*

A PRACTICAL TREATISE ON ORGAN BUILDING. By F. E. ROBERTSON. With Working Drawings and Appendices for ready calculation of all parts. Text in one vol. Demy 8vo, and numerous plates in a royal 4to vol. 2 volumes, 31s. 6d. net.

"Many books upon Organ Building have been published in recent years, but for fulness of information not one approaches Mr. Robertson's work, wherein practical details and directions are given in every department of Organ construction. The book is of course based upon old Don Bedos' famous work, and contains the most valuable portion of Dr. Topfer's German treatise, together with his learned diagrams and illustrations."—HERMANN SMITH'S "The Making of Sound In the Organ and In the Orchestra." W. Reeves.

MODERN ORGAN TUNING, The How and Why, Clearly Explaining the Nature of the Organ Pipe and the System of Equal Temperament, Together with an Historic Record of the Evolution of the Diatonic Scale from the Greek Tetrachord. By HERMANN SMITH. Crown 8vo, cloth, 3s. 6d.

"The greatest authority on acoustical matters connected with organ pipes who has ever lived."—G. A. AUDSLEY in his *Art of Organ Building.*

"I have read 'Modern Organ Tuning' with great interest. It is a book of value and should find appreciative readers. It should be a handbook with students of the organ and organ tuning."—A. J. HIPKINS.

"Simple non-technical terms sets out with an attractiveness and lucidity I have never seen surpassed the history of the evolution of the diatonic scale from the Greek tetrachord * * * by no means intended for organ students alone * * the historical explanations add to the fascination of this volume."—*Daily Telegraph.*

"The book is just such another as its author's similar manual on the tuning of pianos, a workmanlike handbook; full of sound practical advice for the craftsmen concerned."—*Scotsman.*

"Recommended to the notice of organists with the fullest confidence that they would derive both pleasure and profit from its perusal."—*Scottish Guardian.*

RINK'S PRACTICAL ORGAN SCHOOL: A New Edition Carefully Revised. The Pedal Part printed on a Separ ate Staff, and the Preface, Remarks and Technica Terms translated from the German expressly for thi Edition by John Hiles. The Six Books Complete, hand somely bound in red cloth, gilt edges, ob. folio, 10s. 6c net (issued at 20s.), or the six parts 7s. 6d. net (issue at 6s. each), parts sold separately.

The best edition ever published of this Grand Classical work. No oth edition will bear comparison with it for care and skill in editing, nor fc beauty of engraving and excellence of printing. One special merit of th edition is that the *bar lines* are bold, and that they are drawn *right throug the score*, instead of through each staff, as was the custom in days gone b The student who will take the trouble to test this edition against an other, will at once perceive the advantage he gains from this clear an distinct style of "barring"; to an advanced performer the matter may l perhaps of less importance, but even he cannot fail to appreciate the con fort of increased legibility.

As a royal road to thorough and sound Organ Playing in all styles, the is no other School which will bear comparison with this: a Beginn can follow no better course than to go through it slowly.

A SHORT HISTORY OF THE ORGAN, Organists, and Ser vices of the Chapel of Alleyn's College, Dulwich. Wit Extracts from the Diary of the Founder. By W. E Stocks. Crown 8vo, sewed, 1s.

THE EARLY ENGLISH ORGAN BUILDERS and thei Works, from the 15th Century to the Period of the Grea Rebellion. An Unwritten Chapter on the History the Organ. By Dr. E. F. Rimbault. Well printe With woodcuts, post 8vo, cloth, 3s. 6d.

ANALYSIS OF MENDELSSOHN'S ORGAN WORKS. A Study of their Structural Features. For the Use o Students. By Joseph W. G. Hathaway, Mus. B. Oxon. 127 Musical Examples. Portrait and Facsimiles. Crowi 8vo, beveiled cloth, 4s. 6d.

THE MAKING OF SOUND IN THE ORGAN AND IN TH ORCHESTRA. With many illustrations. By Herman Smith. Crown 8vo, cloth, 7s. 6d. *In the Press.*

Highly recommended by the late A. J. Hipkins.

ORGANIST'S QUARTERLY JOURNAL of Original Compos tions. Edited by Dr. W. Spark, 5s. per part. Ne Series Volume, 160 large pages, oblong folio, bound i cloth, 18s.

THE ORGAN PARTS OF MENDELSSOHN'S ORATORIOS AND OTHER CHORAL WORKS. Analytically Considered. By ORLANDO A. MANSFIELD, *Mus. Doc., F.R.C.O.* With numerous Musical Examples. Crown 8vo, cloth, 4s. 6d.

HENRY SMART'S ORGAN COMPOSITIONS ANALYSED. By J. BROADHOUSE. Crown 8vo, bevelled cloth, 2s. 6d.

THE INFLUENCE OF THE ORGAN IN HISTORY. By DUDLEY BUCK. New Edition with Illustrations. Crown 8vo, sewed, 1s. net.

CATECHISM for the Harmonium and American Organ. By JOHN HILES. Post 8vo, sewed, 1s.

REFORM IN ORGAN BUILDING. By THOMAS CASSON. Crown 8vo, sewed, 6d

---

THE MUSICAL STANDARD. A Weekly Newspaper for Musicians, Professional and Amateur. Established nearly Half a Century. The Organ of no *Clique*. Independent Criticisms. Correspondents in all Parts of the World. Translations of Important Articles from the foreign musical press. Illustrated Supplement *every week*. "The Violin and String World" given with the number the last Saturday of each month. Price Twopence (by post, 2½d.). Annual Subscription, 10s. 10d., 6 months, 5s. 5d., 3 months, 2s. 9d. (Abroad, 12 months, 13s., 6 months, 6s. 6d.) Terms for Advertisements on application to the Manager. Cases for binding, 1s. 6d. net (by post, 1s. 9d.).

Portraits of celebrated musicians are given from time to time in "The Musical Standard." Price 2d. each. List of Portraits that have already appeared sent post free on application.

PIANOFORTE.

REEVES' VAMPING TUTOR. Art of Extemporaneous Accompaniment, or Playing by Ear on the Pianoforte, Rapidly Enabling anyone having an Ear for Music (with or without any knowledge of Musical Notation) to Accompany with Equal Facility in any Key with Practical Examples. By FRANCIS TAYLOR. New Edition, to which is added Instructions for Accompaniment with Equal Facility in every Key illustrated by Examples. Folio, 2s.

PIANOFORTE TEACHER'S GUIDE. By L. PLAIDY. Translated by FANNY RAYMOND RITTER. Crown 8vo, boards, 1s.

"Evidently written by a pianist who is a thorough master of his instrument as well as a good teacher."—*Educational Times.*

"Some of the finest pianists of the day owe much of their technical facility to Plaidy's excellent method."—*Bazaar.*

"The best possible advice of a veteran; no teacher can read it without benefit. Affixed is a list of studies in order of difficulty. This is especially valuable."—*Schoolmaster.*

THE ART OF TUNING THE PIANOFORTE, A New and Comprehensive Treatise to Enable the Musician to Tune his Pianoforte upon the System founded on the Theory of Equal Temperament. By HERMANN SMITH. Crown 8vo, limp cloth, New Edition, thoroughly Revised, 2s.

Readers will welcome this note of approval signed by A. J. Hipkins, a name long associated with the Pianoforte and familiar to most musicians in the musical literature of the present time. No better voucher could be desired of the fair claims of this little book upon the reader's attention and confidence. "I have had the privilege of reading the proofs of Mr. Hermann Smith's clear and exhaustive treatise on Pianoforte Tuning, and I am satisfied that for the professional tuner, or the amateur who desires to understand the subject and put the knowledge he acquires into practice, there is no book upon it yet published that may be compared with it. I recommend all tuners or would-be tuners to study this unpretending and excellent work, wherein the theory is laid down in clear and correct terms, and the practice, as far as this is possible, is indicated judiciously."

THE DEPPE FINGER EXERCISES for Rapidly Developing an Artistic Touch in Pianoforte Playing, carefully Arranged, Classified and Explained by AMY FAY (Pupil of Tausig, Kullak, Liszt and Deppe). Folio, English Fingering, 1s. 6d. (Continental Fingering, 1s. 6d.)

The *Musical Times* says:—We are asked by a well-known pianist to say that Herr Emil Sauer was trained up to his seventeenth year on the Deppe system and that he owes his wonderful technique almost solely to that method * * * Our correspondent adds that Herr Sauer speaks as enthusiastically of the Deppe method as did Miss Amy Fay.

PIANO TOUCH, PHRASING AND INTERPRETATION. By J. ALFRED JOHNSTONE (*author of* "The Art of Teaching Piano Playing," etc.) Crown 8vo, cloth, 3s. 6d.

CONTENTS:—I. TOUCH IN PIANO-PLAYING AND SOME OF ITS CURIOSITIES. Varied Meanings of the Word "Touch"—"Touch" as Applied to the Instrument—Limitations of "Touch"—Possibilities of "Touch"—Confused Ideas on "Touch"—Tone-Colour—Causes of Confused Ideas—"Touch" as Applied to the General Effect produced by the Player—Objective Results of Subjective Desires. Melody-Playing—Diverse Kinds of "Touch"—Brilliant Legato Passage "Touch"—Two Broad Varieties or Schools of "Touch"—Recommendation of Lucidity. II. ON THE MYSTERY OF PHRASING IN PIANO-PLAYING. The Cant of Phrasing—What is Phrasing?—Clear Perception of the Formal Divisions of Music—The Foundation of Phrasing—Erroneous Notion of Bar to Bar Construction—Appeal made Effective by Intelligible Illustrations—The Right Method of Making Phrase Divisions Clear in Piano-Playing—Motival Phrasing—Expressive Treatment of Phrases. III. HINTS ON THE RIGHT INTERPRETATION OF BACH'S WOLTEMPIRIRTE-CLAVIER ON THE PIANO. Eulogiums of Eminent Musicians—Bach's Conflicting Interpreters—The Simple Rule of the Trusting Disciple—Subjects of Conflicting Opinion—The Text—Interpretation—Clavichord or Harpsichord—Bach's Clavichord Playing—Emotional Element in Bach's Fugues—Clavichord or Piano Interpretation—How to Interpret Polyphonic Music on the Piano—Interpretation Regarded from the Standpoint of Style—Analysis of the Right Foundations for Phrasing—Tempo—Legato; Staccato; Use of Pedal; Time Variations—Interpretation of Bach's Ornaments—Conclusion. IV. EDUCATIONAL EDITIONS OF PIANO CLASSICS. Modern Educational Progress in Music—Some Uses of Good Annotated Editions—Objections to Annotated Editions—Comparative Rank of Piano Classics—Editions of Bach's Woltempirirte-Clavier—Editions of Beethoven's Sonatas—Editions of Chopin's Works—Editions of Mozart, Haydn, Schumann, Mendelssohn—Curiosities of Doctrine on Piano Touch.

How Bach's Fugues should be rightly interpreted on the piano is one which is still at issue. The various opinions on the subject already set forth are here examined, and practical suggestions are made on many aspects of this most interesting question.

"We can unreservedly recommend this book to all musical people who are pianists."—*Cheltenham Examiner.*

"This is a book of rare educational excellence—the work of an expert of acknowledged standing and experience, who possesses not only a very complete knowledge of his subject, but also the faculty of expressing himself in clear and unmistakable terms."—*Aberdeen Daily Journal.*

"Valuable hints on phrasing."—*Freeman's Journal.*

"A thoughtful and instructive discussion of many vexed questions of musical taste and particularly of musical execution, with a special reference to the inner mysteries whereby the piano is made to talk to you."—*Scotsman.*

"Without any difficulty, the author disposes of most of the cant about touch' and shows that the so-called *mystery* is only a matter of proper *technique*. Willingly would I quote from the text, only I think it better for the reader to get the book and go through it quietly, marking his favourite passages for future reference."—*The Musical Star.*

"The aid he gives to the student in search of the best annotated editions of works is invaluable."—*Sheffield Daily Independent.*

"Deals at some length with the technique of pianoforte-playing."—*Yorkshire Post.*

A HANDBOOK TO CHOPIN'S WORKS. Giving a Detaile Account of all the Compositions of Chopin. Shoı Analyses for the Piano Student and Critical Quota tions from the Writings of Well-Known Musicε Authors. By G. C. ASHTON JONSON. The Whol Forming a Complete Guide for Concert-Goers, Pianist and Pianola-Players, also a Short Biography, Criticε Bibliography and a Chronological List of Works, et Crown 8vo, cloth, gilt top, 6s.

Will be found equally useful and helpful to concert-goers, for whom forms a permanent analytical programme, to pianists, and to those am teurs of music who can now, owing to the pianola, pursue for the fir time a systematic and co-ordinated study of Chopin's works, a deligl hitherto denied to them owing to their inability to read or play the mo difficult compositions.

"Here in one compact volume, is all that it is necessary to know abo Chopin and his works except by the leisured enthusiast * * * Each sepa ate opus is placed in its proper sequence, and attached to them are bri extracts, again from very many writings, together with Mr. Ashto Jonson's own lucid criticisms. The task is well done: nothing has a parently been left out that ought to have been put in, and never on can our author be accused of being tedious. The book should be great studied by all."—*Daily Chronicle.*

"We would go further and welcome this carefully compiled handbo in the interests of all musicians."—*Daily Telegraph.*

"It is obvious to us that Mr. Jonson has done exceedingly well, and is to be hoped that the many lovers of Chopin will reward his labours l purchasing his clever, eminently practical and highly interesting aı instructive handbook."—*Musical Standard.*

"A most useful addition to Chopin literature in the English language —*Musical Times.*

"A volume full of interest and instruction, even for those who thi they know their Chopin well already."—*Truth.*

AN ESSAY on the Theory and Practice of Tuning in Genera and on Schiebler's Invention of Tuning Pianofort and Organs by the Metronome in Particular. Tran lated by A. WEHRHAN. Crown 8vo, sewed, 1s.

PRACTICE REGISTER for Pupil's Daily Practice. Specimen, 1d., or 1s. per 100.

In the Press.

THE NATIONAL MUSIC OF THE WORLD. By H. CHORLEY. Edited by H. G. HEWLETT. Contains maı Musical Illustrations. New Edition with Index. Crow 8vo, cloth, 6s. 1910

The subject matter of the above volume is treated of under the di sions of Music from the East, Music from the South, Music from t North, and Music from the West.

WELL-KNOWN PIANO SOLOS. How to Play them with Understanding, Expression and Effect. By CHARLES W. WILKINSON. *First Series.* Containing 26 Articles dealing with the Works of Sinding, Scarlatti, Paderewski, Handel, Rubinstein, Scharwenka, Schumann, Godard, Delibes, etc. Crown 8vo, 1s.

Second and Third Series. Uniform with above. Each dealing with twenty-six various pieces. 1s. each.

Contents of the First Series:—SINDING, Rustle of Spring. SCARLATTI, Pastorale e Capriccio. PADEREWSKI, Minuet in G. HANDEL, Harmonious Blacksmith. RUBINSTEIN, Melody in F. SCHARWENKA, Polish Dance. SCHUMANN, Nachtstücke. GODARD, Mazurka. DELIBES, Pizzicati from Sylvia. GRIEG, Wedding Day at Troldhangen. ELGAR, Salut d'Amour. PADEREWSKI, Melodie. RAFF, La Fileuse. TCHAIKOVSKY, Troika. GODARD, Berger et Bergères. CHAMINADE, Pierrette. MOSZKOWSKI, Etincelles. PADEREWSKI, Minuet in A Major. GRIEG, Norwegian Bridal Procession. LISZT, Regata Veneziana. CHAMINADE, Automne. MOSZKOWSKI, Serenata. LACK, Valse Arabesque. SCHUMANN, Arabeske. CHOPIN, Etude in G Flat. DURAND, First Valse.

Draws one's attention to the beauties in a piece, explains difficulties here and there, draws attention to a pedal effect and any peculiarity of fingering, and generally gives all the information a professor is expected to give to his pupils.

"Described in detail in a manner to be understood by the youngest student, and with a charm that must ensure the popularity of the book." —*Aberdeen Daily Journal.*

TECHNICAL STUDY IN THE ART OF PIANOFORTE PLAYING (Deppe's Principles). By C. A. EHRENFECHTER. With numerous Illustrations. Fourth Edition. Crown 8vo, bevelled cloth, 2s. 6d.

CONTENTS:—Position—Arm—Wrist—Fingers; Touch (Tone Production); Legato; Equality of Tone; Tension and Contraction; Five Finger Exercises; Skips; The Scale; Arpeggio Chords; Firm Chords; High Raising of the Arm; Melody and its Accompaniment; Connection of Firm Chords; The Tremolo; The Shake (Trill); The Pedal; Fingering.

A detailed and exhaustive exposition of Deppe's principles of the Pianoforte technic in all its features, notably with regard to touch and passage playing, showing the immense advantage to be gained by their application, from the elementary to the higher stages of technical development.

A piano-student writes:—"Most useful. I am always re-reading and studying it. It has helped me a lot."

A professional musician who studied after this method, writes in an issue of the *Musical Standard* as follows:—"I am sure many must have felt with me that the old system of teaching was useless for the production of a technique fit to grapple with the appalling difficulties of much of the music of the modern romantic school of composers. Let all whom are ambitious to overcome such difficulties attack them on the lines laid down by C. A. Ehrenfechter, and I am convinced they will find, as I have done, their desires realised in a most astonishing manner."

DELIVERY IN THE ART OF PIANOFORTE PLAYING, On Rhythm, Measure, Phrasing, Tempo. By C. A. EHRENFECHTER. Crown 8vo, bevelled cloth, 2s.

"Deals with rhythm, measure, phrasing and *tempo* as applied to pianoforte playing * * explains the difference between the *subjective* and *objective* in delivery and expresses his opinion that a performance of the *born* artist must of necessity be subjective, while the wavering, undecided, and uninspired amateur will be safest in giving an altogether objective rendering. The section with reference to accent is particularly good. There are numerous illustrations from the works of the masters."—W. H. WEBBE in *The Pianist's A. B. C.*

PIANO TEACHING. Advice to Pupils and Young Teachers. By F. LE COUPPEY (Prof. in the Conservatory of Music, Paris, etc.) Translated from the Third French Edition by M. A. BIERSTADT. Post 8vo, cloth, 2s.

"Well worthy of perusal both by young teachers and pupils. The book contains sound advice, particularly applicable to the study of Pianoforte playing."—W. H. WEBBE in *The Pianist's A. B. C.*

TECHNICAL AND THEORETICAL.

MODERN CHORDS EXPLAINED. (The Tonal Scale in Harmony.) By ARTHUR G. POTTER. With Musical Examples from the Works of C. Debussy, Richard Strauss and Granville Bantock. 8vo, limp cloth, 1s. (paper cover, 6d.)

HOW TO HARMONIZE MELODIES. With Hints on Writing for Strings and Pianoforte Accompaniments. By J. HENRY BRIDGER, *Mus.Bac.* With Musical Examples throughout. Crown 8vo, cloth, 2s. 6d.

The above work deals with a branch of the subject of Harmony which in the past received but scant consideration in the standard treatises; and though of late years works have appeared dealing more or less fully with the subject, there are some points which, as the result of many years' teaching experience, the author considers require to be treated in greater detail to afford the students the necessary guidance; such, for example, as the treatment of the cadences and of accidentals. The present work is an attempt to supply this, and is almost entirely practical.

CHAPTERS: Method of Study—Cadences and Analysis of Melodies—Final Cadences—Middle Cadences—Harmonization with Primary Chords—Dominant Seventh and Secondary Chords—Use of other Diatonic Discords—Florid Melodies—Accidentals, Modulation and Chromatic Chords—Harmonization in Three and Five Parts—Part-Writing for Strings—Adding Free Accompaniments.

EXERCISES IN VOCAL SCORE READING. Collected from the Works of Orlando di Lasso, Palestrina, Vittoria, Barcroft, Redford, Peter Certon, Byrd, Gibbons, Croft, Rogers, Boyce, etc. For Students preparing for the R.C.O. and other Examinations. By JAMES LYON, *Mus.Doc. Oxon.* 4to, paper covers, 3s.

Although there are books on vocal score reading in existence, the author has found the exercises contained in this book—*taken from the works of writers of the early contrapuntal school*—of the greatest possible value in his private teaching, and he ventures to think that students preparing for diplomas where vocal score reading is required, will welcome such a collection as this

EXERCISES IN FIGURED BASS AND MELODY HARMONIZATION. By DR. JAMES LYON. 4to, paper covers, 2s.

EXAMPLES OF FOUR PART WRITING FROM FIGURED BASSES AND GIVEN MELODIES. 4to, paper covers, 4s.

These exercises are printed in open score so as to be of use in score reading tests. This volume forms a key to "Exercises in Figured Bass" by the same author.

HOW TO COMPOSE. A Practical Guide to the Composition of all Works within the Lyric Form, and which include the Valse, Gavotte, Mazurka, Polonaise March, Minuet, and all Ordinary Dance Forms; as also the Nocturne, Impromptu, Berceuse, Reverie and Similar Characteristic Pieces. By EDWIN EVANS SENIOR, *F.R.C.O.* (*author of* "The Relation of Tchaikovsky to Art-Questions of the Day," "A Handbook to Brahms' Works," "The Modal Accompaniment to Plain Chant," etc.). With 60 Musical Examples Crown 8vo, cloth, 2s. 6d. (paper, 1s. 6d. net).

This work is a store of the most valuable and practical musical knowledge, so condensed as to be of immense utility for its purpose.

The plan adopted is that of gradually developing a full composition under the reader's own observation; and of explaining to him every feature as it occurs in such plain terms that the merest average musical knowledge is alone required for its comprehension. The principles of this little book are in complete accord with those of the very highest authorities; and full indices have been provided in order to bring every fact of its contents within instant reach. Independently of composition it is of special interest to the general reader; whilst to the musician and student it is invaluable. This work is based upon the analogy of the above to lyrical poetry; advantage being taken of the reader's knowledge of the latter.

"A daring subject to tackle, and one that in most cases would be better left alone. We must confess that we opened the book feeling very sceptical; but the author—who is well known as one of the most thoughtful of our musical *litterateurs*—has handled his subject in a manner that compels our admiration. To the young musician who feels that he has something to say, we strongly advise the immediate purchase of this thoughtful and distinctly practical treatise. It will save him from that loose, meandering, formless music so characteristic, unfortunately, of many of the early works of our young composers."—*Aberdeen Daily Journal.*

PRONOUNCING DICTIONARY OF MUSICAL TERMS. By DR. DUDLEY BUCK. Sixth Edition, with the Pronunciation of each Term accurately given. Edited and Revised by A. WHITTINGHAM. Crown 8vo, cloth, 1s. (paper, 6d.)

A most valuable and useful little book to all musical people. The method adopted for giving the correct pronunciation of each term is most concise and clear.

HARMONY, EASILY AND PROGRESSIVELY ARRANGED. Presenting in a Simple Manner the Elementary Ideas as well as the Introduction to the Study of Harmony. With about 300 Musical Examples and Exercises. By PAUL COLBERG. Crown 8vo, cloth, 2s. (paper, 1s.)

August Wilhelmj says:—"This work is distinguished by brevity and clearness I most warmly recommend it."

THE RUDIMENTS OF GREGORIAN MUSIC. By FRANCIS BURGESS, *F.S.A., Scot.* Crown 8vo, 6d.

Plainsong or Gregorian Music, is the generic name given to that great system of ecclesiastical melody formulated by the primitive Church and retained in later ages as the official chant for use during the most solemn acts of Christian worship. As a system it represents the accumulated knowledge of several centuries usually accounted great by those who respect tradition and whilst its peculiar and characteristic solemnity marks it out as an ideal form of sacred music which the modern composer may study with profit.

"An entertaining and instructive brochure."—*Burton Daily Mail.*

"A very clear and concise treatise."—*Liverpool Daily Post.*

EXERCISES ON GENERAL ELEMENTARY MUSIC. A Book for Beginners. By K. PAIGE. Fourth Edition, Part I. Price 9d. Part II., price 1s. Crown 8vo, sewed (2 parts complete in cloth, 2s. 4d.)

CONTENTS of PART I.—1. Pitch. 2. Length of Sounds. 3. Time. 4. Time and Accent. 5. Intervals. 6. Scales. 7. Transposition. 8. Syncopation. 9. Signs and Abbreviations. 10. Notation. 11. Miscellaneous Questions and Exercises.

CONTENTS of PART II.—1. Triads. 2. First Inversion of a Triad. 3. Second Inversion of a Triad. 4. Dissonances. 5. Suspensions. 6. Sequences. 7. Cadences. 8. Dominant Sevenths, etc., etc.

"We have much praise not only for the general arrangement of the book, but for the lucid manner in which the questions are put. The Chapters on Time and Accent are exceedingly good, and there are some useful exercises to accustom the pupil to transposition. We are especially pleased, too, with the method of writing incomplete bars, and asking the pupil to supply the missing parts with rests: also of requiring notes to be changed into rests and rests into notes."—*Musical Times.*

THE ART OF MODULATING. A Series of Papers on Modulating at the Pianoforte. By HENRY C. BANISTER. With 62 Musical Examples. Crown 8vo, limp cloth, 2s.

Moreover in writing a composition there is time to think, devise and contrive; but that which is the subject of the above work is promptness, readiness, and quick thought under special circumstances.

Not only at examinations—*viva voce*—but in actual experience, is ability required to pass rapidly with very little "process" from one key to another.

"A great portion of the book is taken up with analyses of the modulations employed by the great composers in their most significant works—these are always scholarly and ingenious and certainly show how by practice wedded to adequate knowledge it may be possible to pass rapidly with very little of what the writer calls 'process' from one key to another."—*London Musical Courier.*

THE STUDENT'S BOOK OF CHORDS. By PASCAL NEEDHAM. Crown 8vo, sewed, 6d.

The Author says:—A very large number of music students, executive and theoretical, have expressed to me from time to time a desire for a cheap book, in which the chords with their inversions and resolutions are briefly and clearly explained. To these students I dedicate this work.

ELEMENTARY MUSIC. A Book for Beginners. By Dr Westbrook. With Questions and Vocal Exercises Thirteenth Edition. Crown 8vo, cloth, 1s. 6d. (paper 1s.)

Contents:—1. The Staff and its Clefs. 2. Notes and their Rests. Bars and Time. 4. Accidentals. 5. Keys and Scales. 6. Intervals. Musical Pitch. 8. Accent. 9. Secondary Signs. 10. Ornaments and Grou of Notes. 11. Voices and Scores. 12. Church Modes. 13. Italian and oth Directions. 14. Foreign Note-Names. 15. Questions. 16. Vocal Exercises

"His explanations are extremely clear. The questions at the end wi be found very useful."—*Musical Times.*

"This little primer is one of the best of its kind, and forms an admi able course of preparation for the local examinations in music * * * * ensures, as far as a book can, an intelligent and thorough grasp of tl elements of musical knowledge. The questions at the end of the book wi be found invaluable to teachers."—*Journal of Trinity College, London.*

HOW TO MEMORIZE MUSIC. By C. F. Kenyon. Wit numerous Musical Examples. Crown 8vo, cloth, 2 (paper, 1s.)

"Mr. Kenyon proves himself an excellent guide; and indeed we kno of no other work devoted to the subject with which he has dealt so tho oughly and so successfully."—*Glasgow Herald.*

"Points out the paramount importance of being able to play fro memory. Many useful hints are given on the course of study to l adopted."—*Morning Post.*

"A most valuable little book of eight chapters, containing valuab information on the art of memorising, with many illustrations."—*Weste Morning News.*

"May do much good inducing young pianists to exert their brains t gether with their fingers."—*Yorkshire Post.*

HARMONY AND THE CLASSIFICATION OF CHORD With Questions and Exercises. By Dr. J. H. Lewi Vol. 1, 8vo, boards, cloth back, 5s.

——— *Ditto*, Vol. 2. 8vo, boards, cloth back, 5s.

COUNTERPOINT: A Simple and Intelligible Treatise. Co taining the most Important Rules of all Text Books, i Catechetical Form; (Forming an Answer to the Questio "What is Counterpoint?") Intended for Beginner By A. Livingstone Hirst. Crown 8vo, sewed, 9d.

THE ART OF MODULATION. A Hand-book Showing at Glance the Modulations from one Key to any Other i the Octave, consisting of 1,008 Modulations. For th Use of Organists and Musical Directors Edited b Carli Zoeller. Third Editi Roy. 8vo, cloth, 4 (paper, 2s. 6d.)

THE HARMONISING OF MELODIES. A Text-Book for Students and Beginners. By H. C. BANISTER. Third Edition, with numerous Musical Examples. Crown 8vo, limp cloth, 2s.

CHAPTERS:—Introductory, The Resources of Harmony; Harmonising with Common Chords Only, General Principles. Couplets of Common Chords; Plan, Rhythmical Structure, Phrases, Cadences; Cadences in Connection with Modulation, Melodies in the Minor Mode, Continuity, Congruity with Words; Illustrations of Harmonising the same Melody in Different Ways with Changed Mode; Florid Melodies, Unessential Notes, Different Forms of Harmonising; Pianoforte Accompaniment to a Melody; Arpeggio Accompaniment; Accidentals and Chromatic Passing Notes, A Caution, Summary.

MUSICAL SHORTHAND for Composers, Students of Harmony, Counterpoint, etc., can be Written very Rapidly and is more Legible than printed Music, with Specimens from Bach, Handel, Chopin, Wagner, Mendelssohn, Spohr, Mozart, etc. By FRANCIS TAYLOR, 14 pages, 12mo, sewed, 6d.

"Composers and Students of Music expend a vast amount of time in mere painful mechanism." We have only six totally unlike signs. These from their simplicity can be written with great rapidity, one dip of the pen sufficing for an entire page, and the writing being as legible as possible.—*Preface.*

TRANSPOSITION AT SIGHT. For Students of the Organ and Pianoforte. By H. ERNST NICHOL. Third Edition, with numerous Musical Exercises. Crown 8vo, cloth, 1s. 6d. (paper, 1s.)

There is no need to dwell upon the usefulness or even the necessity of transposition to the organist or the accompanist of songs. The practice of transposing upon the lines here laid down developes the "mental ear," quickens the musical perception and gives ease in sight-reading; as it is evident that, if the student can *transpose* at sight, he will not have much difficulty in merely *playing* at sight. The author has made free use of the tonic sol-fa as well as the old notation in his many musical examples.

MUSICAL ANALYSIS. A Handbook for Students. By H. C. BANISTER. With Musical Illustrations. Crown 8vo, limp cloth, 2s.

This series of Papers has not been intended as a Treatise on its boundless subject; only illustrative of the way in which students may go to work in the interesting process of Analysis. To work at it is much more interesting and improving than to read Analysis already made for them. The student should look out for beauties, even of the simpler kind, as well as endeavour to solve recondite problems. Try and enjoy the landscape and not merely map out the country.

"This neatly-got-up volume is indispensable to all students of music. It is at once thorough and popular, scientific and interesting, and whilst most instructive, it is charmingly luminous."—*Gentleman's Journal.*

THE STUDENT'S HELMHOLTZ. Musical Acoustics or the Phenomena of Sound as Connected with Music. By JOHN BROADHOUSE. With more than 100 Illustrations. Fourth Edition. Crown 8vo, cloth, 7s. 6d.

"In his Preface the author says:—'The object of the present book is to give, in one volume, a good general view of the subject to those who can neither spare time to read, nor money to buy a number of large and expensive works.' A perusal of the book justifies us in asserting that this design is most satisfactorily carried out; and it is not too much to say that although the plan of the work excludes the possibility of minutely dissecting every subject treated upon, any careful reader may obtain so clear an insight into the principle of acoustics, as to enable him not only to pass an examination but to store up a large amount of general knowledge upon the phenomena of sound."—*Musical Times.*

"The Student's Helmholtz will be very useful to many musicians, to whom much in Helmholtz's work must appear obscure. I shall recommend the book whenever an opportunity offers itself."—DR. RITTER.

This work has been specially designed for musical students preparing for examination.

A FIRST BOOK OF MUSIC FOR BEGINNERS, Embodying Recent English and Continental Teaching. By ALFRED WHITTINGHAM. Sixth Thousand. Crown 8vo, sewed, 2d.

The two principal objects kept in view in writing this little book were Thoroughness of Definition and Regular Order in the arrangement of Subjects. It differs from all other similar works in that all the technical terms in music are introduced in the Answers not in the Questions.

VIOLIN.

THE VIOLIN AND OLD VIOLIN MAKERS. Being a Historical and Biographical Account of the Violin. By A. MASON CLARKE. With Facsimiles of Labels used by Old Masters and illustrations of a copy of a Gasparo da Salo. Crown 8vo, cloth, 2s. net (paper, 1s. net).

The Author in his Preface says: "I set to work with the object of presenting in a concise form such information as I have thought necessary, or at least of interest to every one who elects to take up the violin, either as an object of recreation or serious study. In order to facilitate my labours, I have consulted the leading British and foreign authorities on the violin and kindred instruments. I have also during many years devoted much time to the inspection and study of genuine old instruments."

CONTENTS: Part I.—Historical. 1. Introductory and Early English 2. Italy. 3. France. 4. Germany. Part II.—Biographical Violin Makers of the Old School. 1. Italian, with Labels. 2. German and Tyrolese, with Labels. 3. French, with Labels. 4. British, with Label. Part III.—On the Development of Classical Music for the Violin and other Stringed Instruments.

THE ART OF HOLDING THE VIOLIN AND BOW AS EXEMPLIFIED BY OLE BULL. His Pose and Method proved to be based on true Anatomical Principles. By A. B. CROSBY, *M.D., Professor of Anatomy.* Portrait, Diagrams and Illustrations. 8vo, cloth, 2s. (paper, 1s.)

Included in the above are some interesting recollections and anecdotes of Ole Bull.

THE VIOLIN AND STRING WORLD. Monthly (in Continuation of "The Violin Times.") With Portrait Supplements. Annual Subscription 2s. 6d. (Abroad 3s.)

SKETCHES OF GREAT VIOLINISTS AND GREAT PIANISTS. See "Biographical Section."

LIFE OF STRADIVARIUS. See "Biographical Section."

BIOGRAPHICAL DICTIONARY OF FIDDLERS. See "Biographical Section."

VIOLIN MANUFACTURE IN ITALY and its German Origin. By DR. E. SCHEBEK. Translated by W. E. LAWSON. Second Edition. Square 12mo, sewed, 1s.

HOW TO REPAIR VIOLINS and other Musical Instruments. By ALFRED F. COMMON. With Diagrams. Crown 8vo, cloth, 2s. (paper, 1s.)

TECHNICS OF VIOLIN PLAYING. By KARL COURVOISIER. With Illustrations. Tenth Edition. Cloth, 2s. 6d (paper, 1s.)

"It is my opinion that this book will offer material aid to all violin players."—JOACHIM.

"As far as words, aided by diagrams, can make clear so practical a subject as the playing of a musical instrument, this little book leave nothing to be desired. The author, who was a pupil of Joachim, has treated the subject in a most thorough manner, and we can highly recommend his little book."—*Educational Times.*

"Illustrated in the clearest possible manner, by really admirable drawings."—*Graphic.*

"Courvoisier, a pupil of Joachim, has aimed at presenting an exposition of the methods of that great master, in which attempt he has, according to Herr Joachim's own explicit declaration, been very successful."—*Scotsman.*

"A most thorough exposition of everything connected with this difficult instrument."—*Schoolmaster.*

TREATISE ON THE STRUCTURE AND PRESERVATION OF THE VIOLIN and all other Bow Instruments. Together with an Account of the most Celebrated Makers and of the Genuine Characteristics of their Instruments By J. A. OTTO, with Additions by J. BISHOP. With Diagrams and Plates. Fourth Edition, further Enlarged. Crown 8vo, cloth, 3s.

Contains instructions for the repair, preservation and bringing out the tone of instruments; tracing model for violin, mutes and fiddle holders list of classical works for stringed instruments. This work is especially valuable for makers of violins.

HOW TO PLAY THE FIDDLE. For Beginners on the Violin. By H. W. and G. GRESSWELL. Eighth Edition. Crown 8vo, cloth, 2s. (paper, 1s.)

JOACHIM says:—"Contains many useful hints about violin playing."

CONTENTS:—General and Introductory—On Teaching the Violin—On Instruction Books—On Practice—Relating to the Purchase of a Violin—Importance of Buying a Good One—How to Set about Securing a good Violin—The Merits of Old Fiddles, Age and Use—The Testing or Making Trial of a Fiddle—Preservation and Repair of Violins—General and Historical—Few Short Remarks of a General Character—Short History of Some Celebrated Violin Makers—The Sound Bar and the Sound Post—The Bridge—A Few Words on the Pegs, Mute, Resin and Fingerboard—The Strings—The Mode of Stringing—The Bow—Bowing—The Method of Tuning the Violin—Some Rules to be Observed in Playing—Double Stopping—Harmonics—Remarks on the Shift—The Shake—On Playing with an Accompaniment—Concluding Observations.

"We can cordially recommend this clever little work to all who are studying the violin."—*Graphic.*

FACTS ABOUT FIDDLES. Violins Old and New. By J BROADHOUSE. Fourth Edition. Crown 8vo, sewed, 6d.

THE HISTORY OF THE VIOLIN and other Instruments Played on with the Bow from the Remotest Times to the Present. Also an Account of the Principal Makers, English and Foreign. With Coloured Frontispiece and numerous Full-page Illustrations and Cuts. By WILLIAM SANDYS, F.S.A., and SIMON ANDREW FORSTER. 390 pages, 8vo, cloth, 7s. 6d. net (published at 14s.)

THE VIOLIN, Its History and Construction. Illustrated and Described from all Sources. Together with a List of Tyrolese and Italian Makers. With Twenty-nine Illustrations and Folding Example of the First Music Issued for the Lute, Viol and Voice. From the German. of ABELE and NIEDERHEITMAN. By JOHN BROADHOUSE. Crown 8vo, cloth, 2s.

"The learned and instructive treatise of Abele, skilfully rendered by J. Broadhouse and supplemented by a version of Niederheitmann's list of Italian and Tyrolese violin makers, a compilation invaluable to collectors and connoisseurs of rare fiddles * * * a work which forms a noteworthy addition to the small number of English books upon this interesting subject."—*Scotsman.*

The importance of this work has been long recognised on the Continent, where it is eagerly sought for at a high price. The above is a full translation, special attention has been given to a proper rendering of technical portions.

INFORMATION FOR PLAYERS, Owners, Dealers and Makers of Bow Instruments, Also for String Manufacturers. Taken from Personal Experiences, Studies and Observations. By WILLIAM HEPWORTH. With Illustrations of Stainer and Guarnerius Violins and Guage of Millimetres and Centimetres, etc. Crown 8vo, cloth, 2s. 6d.

CONTENTS:—The Pegs—Neck—Fingerboard—Bridge—Tail-Piece—Saddle—Violin Holder—Tail-pin—Bar—Sound Post—On the Stringing of Bow Instruments in General Use—Strings—Rosin—Cleaning of the Instrument and the Bridge—Bow—Violin Case—Repairs—Preservation—Conclusion.

HOW TO MAKE A VIOLIN, Practically Treated. By J. BROADHOUSE. New and Revised Edition. With 47 Illustrations and Folding Plates and many Diagrams, Figures, etc. Crown 8vo, bevelled cloth, 3s. 6d.

CONTENTS:—Introduction—The Parts of the Violin—On the Selection of Wood—The Tools Required—The Models—The Mould—The Side-pieces and Side Linings—The Back—Of the Belly—The Thickness of the Back and Belly—The Bass Bar—The Purfling—The Neck—The Finger-Board—The Nut and String Guard—Varnishing and Polishing—Varnishes and Colouring Matter—The Varnish—A Mathematical Method of Constructing the Outline—The Remaining Accessories of the Violin.

This new edition has had the advantage of being revised throughout by a celebrated violin maker.

VOCAL.

THE THROAT IN ITS RELATION TO SINGING. A Series of Popular Papers. By WHITFIELD WARD, A.M., M.D. With Illustrations. Crown 8vo, cloth, 2s. (paper, 1s.).

CONTENTS: Anatomical Structure of the Throat; What we see with the Laryngoscope; How we Sing; How we Breathe; How to take Care of the Voice; Hints to Voice Builders; How the Voice is Destroyed; Common Throat Affections of Singers, together with their Treatment, etc.

TWELVE LESSONS ON BREATHING AND BREATH CONTROL. For Singers, Speakers and Teachers. By GEO E. THORP. Crown 8vo, limp cloth, 1s.

TWENTY LESSONS ON THE DEVELOPMENT OF THE VOICE. For Singers, Speakers and Teachers. By GEO. E. THORP. Crown 8vo, limp cloth, 1s.

Mr. Thorp's two books have from time to time been recommended by various eminent vocal specialists as giving practical aid and advice for the training, care and development of the voice. They are free from any *biased "system" or "discovery."*

TREATISE ON THE TRAINING OF BOY'S VOICES. With Examples and Exercises and Chapters on Choir-Organization. Compiled for the Use of Choirmasters. By GEORGE T. FLEMING. Crown 8vo, cloth, 2s.

GRADUATED COURSE OF EXERCISES FOR BOY CHORISTERS. With Pianoforte Accompaniment. For Use in Conjunction with Above. By G. T. FLEMING. 4to, album, sewed, 1s.

——— *Ditto*, Boy's Voice Part only, 6d.

50 **MUSICAL HINTS TO CLERGYMEN.** Management of Breath, Classification of Male Voices, Management of the Voice, The Service. With twenty specially written Exercises. By GEO. F. GROVER. Crown 8vo, sewed, 1s.

SOME FAMOUS SONGS. An Art Historical Sketch. By F. R. RITTER. 8vo, sewed, 1s.

HOW TO MANAGE A CHORAL SOCIETY. By N. KILBURN, Mus. Bac. Third Edition, Revised. Crown 8vo, sewed, 6d.

HOW TO SING AN ENGLISH BALLAD. By E. PHILP, Seventh Edition. Crown 8vo, sewed, 6d.

"It would be difficult to find a casket of brighter gems than those which lie within the cover of this little work."—*Illustrated London News.*

PHYSICAL DEVELOPMENT IN RELATION TO PERFECT VOICE PRODUCTION. By H. TRAVERS ADAMS, B.A. 8vo, sewed, 2s. net.

This work is especially intended for students and is divided into sections, such as Vibration, Breaks and Registers, The Speaking Voice, Attack, Practical Application, Breathing, Inspiration, Final Exercise in Inspiration, Expiration, Active or Forced Inspiration, Completion of Breathing, Practice of Sounds, Placing, Classification of Voices.

OBSERVATIONS ON THE FLORID SONG. Or Sentiments on the Ancient and Modern Singers. By P. F. TOSI. Translated by MR. GALLIARD. With folding Musical Examples. 184 pages. A Reprint of this Celebrated Book, first published in 1743. Crown 8vo, boards with vellum-like back, price 5s. (pub. 10s).

Recommended to all Students of the Italian Method of Singing by the late Charles Lunn.

" The readers of the *Etude* have frequently been treated to quotations from this remarkable work. To the teacher and student of singing it has a peculiar message. It stands for all that is sound and final in the philosophy of singing and shows that the æsthetics and morals of the art are changeless. Those who need a healthful mental stimulus should read this reprint of a work that represents the best thought and practice of the old Italian singers and singing masters."—*The Etude.*

" It is a practical treatise on singing in which the aged teacher embodies his own experience and that of his contemporaries at a time when the art was probably more thoroughly taught than it has ever been since. Many of its remarks would still be highly useful."—*Grove's Dictionary of Music and Musicians.*

CATECHISM OF PART SINGING. And the Choral Services. By JOHN HILES. Third Edition. Thick post 8vo, sewed, price 1s.

Advice to singers on every point of interest in reference to the vocal organs.

VOICE PRODUCTION AND VOWEL ENUNCIATION. By F. F. MEWBURN LEVIEN. Diagrams by ARTHUR C. BEHREND. Post 8vo, sewed, 6d.

VOCAL EXERCISES FOR CHOIRS AND SCHOOLS. By DR. WESTBROOK. Post 8vo, sewed, 2d.

RUDIMENTS OF VOCAL MUSIC. With 42 Preparatory Exercises, Rounds and Songs in the Treble Clef. By T. MEE PATTISON. Second Edition. Post 8vo, sewed, 2d.

WAGNER.

JUDAISM IN MUSIC (Das Judenthum in der Musik). Being the Original Essay together with the Later Supplement. By RICHARD WAGNER. Translated from the German and Furnished with Explanatory Notes and Introduction. By E. EVANS, *Senior*. Crown 8vo, cloth, 3s. 6d.

CONTENTS: Part I.—THE ORIGINAL ESSAY OF 1850. Chapter I. INTRODUCTORY. The Question introduced. Limitation to Art-Matters. Liberal tendency of modern thought. Its effects. The Jew's introduction to Art. The oppressions of Judaism. Chapter II. CHARACTERISTICS. The Jew's characteristics generally. His exterior. His speech. His artistic incapacities. His mannerisms. His vocal attempts. Chapter III. ART-RELATIONS. Plastic art. The ennoblement of money. Origin disdained. The true poet. The Jewish musician. Absolute music and its Jewish imitation. The Folk-spirit. Chapter IV. MUSICAL CREATION. No Jewish art. Only source of inspiration. Music in the Synagogue. Our Folk-song unavailable. The inner life of our music. The Jewish composer. Chapter V. MENDELSSOHN. Endowments. Bearing of his case upon the subject. Characteristics of his music. The language of Bach. The language of Beethoven. Resumé. Chapter VI. MEYERBEER. General view. Summary of his case. Its relation to our present art-life. Reasons for Jewish appearance in the field of music. EPILOGUE. The Poet Heine and Börne the Author. Part II. THE SUPPLEMENT OF 1869. BEING AN ACCOUNT OF EVENTS SUBSEQUENT TO THE ORIGINAL PUBLICATION. Chapter VII. THE OPENING PHASE OF HOSTILITIES. Tribute to Franz Brendel. The pseudonym of K. Freigedank. The enemy's forces arrayed. The tactics employed. Developments in the Press. Nicknames. Dr. Hanslick on the "Beautiful in Music." His appearance as musical critic. Chapter VIII. THE LISZT PHASE. The new party and Franz Liszt. "Zukunftsmusiker." Secrecy of the enemy's tactics. Liszt's persecution in the Press. Chapter IX. THE THEATRES. Experiences in France, England and Russia. Difficulties created for the later operas. Specialities in hostility. Chapter X. THE NEW ÆSTHETES. Feebleness of the present art-spirit. Lethargy of the new Æsthetes. Their negative zeal. The position of the German composer. Chapter XI. SCHUMANN AND BRENDEL. First impulses. Leading musical characteristic of the period. Robert Schumann. His conversion. First impulses revived by Franz Brendel. Chapter XII. APOSTROPHE. The triumph of Judaism. The present position. Impediments to a closer friendship. Aspirations. Conclusion. Note (On the Author's subsequent view).

BAYREUTH AND MUNICH. A Travelling Record of German Operatic Art. By VERNON BLACKBURN. Crown 8vo, stiff boards, 1s. net.

1. The Philosophy of "Parsifal." 2. Back to a busy World. 3. Munich the Moderate. 4. "Die Zauberflöte." 5. Wagner plus Mozart. 6. A Digression. 7. Back to Bayreuth. 8. Finally Munich: from Two Aspects.

THREE IMPRESSIONS OF BAYREUTH. The 1908 and Previous Wagner Festivals. By ROSE KOENIG. With Two Facsimile Programmes. Crown 8vo, cloth, 2s. net (paper, 1s. net).

"Entertaining and agreeable reading, as recording the impressions of a musical and susceptible hearer."—*Yorkshire Post.*

HOW TO UNDERSTAND WAGNER'S "RING OF THE NIBELUNG." Being the Story and a Descriptive Analysis of the "Rheingold," the "Valkyr," "Siegfried" and the "Dusk of the Gods." With a number of Musical Examples. By GUSTAVE KOBBE. Sixth Edition. Post 8vo, bevelled cloth, gilt top, 3s. 6d.

To be appreciated in the smallest way Wagner must be studied in advance.

WAGNER. "Der Ring des Nibelungen." Being the story concisely told of "Das Rheingold," "Die Walküre," "Siegfried" and "Götterdämmerung." By N. KILBURN. Crown 8vo, sewed, 9d. net.

WAGNER. A Sketch of his Life and Works. By N. KILBURN. Sewed, 6d.

WAGNER'S "PARSIFAL." And the Bayreuth Fest-Spielhaus. By N. KILBURN. Crown 8vo, sewed, 6d.

BEETHOVEN. By RICHARD WAGNER. See "Biographical" tral Section."

ON CONDUCTING. By RICHARD WAGNER. See "Orchestral" Section.

WAGNER. See "Makers of Music." ("Biographical Sect.")
" See "Mezzotints in Modern Music." (Æsthetics, etc., Section.)

MANUSCRIPT MUSIC PAPER.

(*a*) 12 Staves. Roy. 8vo (10 by 6½). Ruled even (120 sheets), the lot 2s. 6d.

This is pre-eminently the Musical Students' Paper, as it is light, portable, smooth and easy to write upon; each sheet, too, will hold a large quantity of matter. There is no paper better suited for Exercises of Counterpoint and Harmony.

(*b*) 12 Staves. Oblong folio (14 by 10). Ruled in groups of 3 Staves for Organ Music. 5 quires (120 sheets), the lot 5s.

The paper is of the same size as ordinary oblong folio, Organ Music *e.g.*, Best's Arrangements, etc.

(*c*) 12 Staves. Folio music size ruled in threes (10 by 14). 5 quires (120 sheets), the lot, 5s.

Exactly the same in size as ordinary folio printed music so that upon it Songs or Organ Pieces may be written just as they are to be printed. It is a very useful paper, as Manuscript music written on it can be bound with Printed Music.

(*d*) 12 Staves. Quarto size (11¾ by 9¼). 5 quires (120 sheets), the lot, 3s. 6d.

(*e*) 12 Staves. Oblong quarto (9¼ by 11¾). 5 quires (120 sheets), the lot 3s. 6d.

(*f*) 12 Staves. Folio music size, ruled even (10 by 14) 5 quires (120 sheets), the lot 5s.

(*g*) 12 Staves. Folio music size, full score, 24 staves (10 by 14). 5 quires (120 sheets), the lot 5s.

(*h*) 14 Staves. Quarto size (11¾ by 9¼). 5 quires (120 sheets), the lot 3s. 6d.

MANUSCRIPT MUSIC BOOKS. Quarto size, 6d.: Octavo size, 6d. and 3d.; Brass Band books, 3d.; Exercise book oblong, 4d.

CHOIR ATTENDANCE REGISTER.

No. 1. Ruled for a Choir of 20 or less for One Year beginning at any date. 1s. 6d.

No. 2. Ruled for a Choir of 40 or less, for One Year beginning at any date. 2s.

No. 3. Ruled for a Choir of 60 or less, for One Year beginning at any date. 2s. 6d.

CHOIR LISTS FOR SUNDAY SERVICES.

No. 1. Morn. and Even. Printed in Red. 1s. 4d. per 100.
No. 2. Morn., Aft. & Even. Printed in Red. 1s. 6d. per 100
No. 3. Morn. & Even. Printed Red & Black. 1s. 8d. per 100
No. 4. Morn. and Even. Printed in Red. 1s. 4d. per 100.

THE ART OF TEACHING PIANOFORTE PLAYING. A Systematised Selection of Practical Suggestions for Young Teachers and Students. By J. ALFRED JOHNSTONE. Author of "Piano Touch, Phrasing and Interpretation," "Modern Tendencies and Old Standards in Musical Art," etc. Thick crown 8vo, cloth, 5s.

Many pianists who add to concert playing the labours of a teacher: many young students about to enter upon the duties of the teaching profession as their life's labour; and indeed, not a few of those who have spent years at the work of giving lessons in pianoforte playing, fail to achieve the success their abilities deserve, simply for the lack of some clear, systematic practical knowledge of the art of teaching. In this volume methods are suggested, hints are offered, principles and rules are formulated, courses of study are sketched out; and all these are sufficiently general and varied to furnish a useful guide for the teacher without circumscribing his individual genius or running any risk of stunting his development.

CONTENTS: Chapter I.—INTRODUCTORY, GENERAL OUTLINE OF THE MINIMUM OF SUBJECTS, DIRECT AND COLLATERAL, INCLUDED IN A LIBERAL MUSICAL EDUCATION. Section I: 1. Technique: what it Means—2. The Necessity for Technique—3. Best System of Technique—4. Various Branches of Technique—5. Protest against "Studies"—6. Advocacy of Purely Technical Exercises—7. Fantastic Theories of Touch. Section II: Interpretation. Section III: Theoretical Subjects—*(a)* The Elements of Music—*(b)* Harmony—*(c)* Form and Analysis—*(d)* Conclusion. Chapter II.—GENERAL SUGGESTIONS FOR TEACHING TECHNIQUE. Section I.—Technical Exercises: 1. Finger Technique—2. Mental Concentration and Co-ordination of Brain and Muscle—3. Position of Hand and Striking Finger—4. Relative Merits of Striking and Pushing the Keys—5. Details of Position—6. Details of Striking—7. A Firm Touch or Full Key Depression—8. Two-Finger Exercises and Finger Gymnastics—9. Three-Finger Exercises—10. Five-Finger Exercises—11. Scale Work—12. The Metronome and Scale Rhythms—13-14. Broken Chords—15. Extended Arpeggios—16. Wrist and Arm Technique—17. Daily Schools of Technical Exercises—18. Some Useful Works on Technique. Section II.—Pianoforte Studies: 1. Introductory Suggestions—2. Progressive Schools of Studies—3. Lists of Graded Studies with Authors and Opus Numbers—4. Octave Studies. Chapter III.—GENERAL SUGGESTIONS FOR TEACHING INTERPRETATION. 1. Introductory Remarks—2. Time and Tempo—3. How to Teach Strict Time—4. Metrical Accentuation—5. Expressive Time Freedom; Quasi Tempo Rubato—6. Parenthetical Note on Slurring—7. Conventional Tempo Rubato—8. How to Teach Accent, Emphasis and Rhythm—9. Rhythm of Divided Beats—10. How to Teach Expressive Freedom in Accentuation—11. Crescendo, Diminuendo and the Various Degrees of Tone-Shading—12. General Suggestions for Teaching Phrasing—13. Monophonic and Polyphonic Music—14. Polyphonic Music—15. How to Teach the Use of the Pedal—16. Character and Style in Interpretation—17. Some Useful Books on Interpretation. Chapter IV.—SUGGESTIONS FOR TEACHING FINGERING, READING, ACCOMPANYING, MEMORISING AND EAR TRAINING. 1. Fingering—2. Uses and Abuses of Reading and Memorising—3. Special Suggestions for Teaching Reading—4. Concise Hints for Reading—5. Accompanying. Chapter V.—GENERAL SUGGESTIONS FOR TEACHING ELEMENTS OF MUSIC, HARMONY AND FORM. 1. Elements—2. Harmony—3. Form—4. Some Useful Books on the Subjects Treated in this Chapter. Chapter VI.—GENERAL SUGGESTIONS FOR EFFECTIVE WORK AT THE LESSON; AND FOR THE WISE DIRECTION OF THE PUPIL'S PRACTICE. Chapter VII.—GENERAL GUIDANCE ON THE CHOICE OF MUSIC, WITH SOME HINTS UPON EDUCATIONAL EDITIONS OF PIANOFORTE CLASSICS. Chapter VIII.—CONCLUDING SUMMARY OF ESSENTIAL POINTS OF VIEW REQUIRING SPECIAL EMPHASIS.

Continued from page 2.

ORGAN BUILDING UP-TO-DATE. An Important Work Especially dealing with Pneumatic Organs. By T. and W. LEWIS. With numerous full page and other smaller Illustrations throughout the Text all drawn to Scale. 4to, cloth.

HANDBOOK TO THE VOCAL WORKS OF BRAHMS. A Historical and Descriptive Account and Complete Analysis of every Vocal Work of Brahms. Treated in the Order of their Opus Numbers. With many Original Translations of the Words. By EDWIN EVANS, SENR. Thick 8vo, cloth.

A COMPARATIVE VIEW OF THE DEVELOPMENT OF OPERA IN ITALY, GERMANY, FRANCE AND ENGLAND. By JOSEPH GODDARD. Showing the Cause of the Falling Back of the English School in the Modern Period; and the Compensation which that Falling Back Involved. With numerous Musical Examples.

SOME CONTINENTAL ORGANS. Ancient and Modern. With Descriptions and Specifications. By JAMES I. WEDGEWOOD.

Printed by The New Temple Press, 17 Grant Road, Croydon. 1000—8—10.

CPSIA information can be obtained
at www.ICGtesting.com
Printed in the USA
BVHW04s1132310818
526159BV00016B/502/P

9 781527 856936